The
Illustrated
GOLF
RULES
Dictionary

Hadyn Rutter

TRIUMPH
BOOKS
CHICAGO

to every golfer who ever wondered
'What do I do in this situation?' –
and to my golfing guru Jim Long –
whose indefatigable energy and
enthusiasm contributed substantially
to this book

Published in North America by
Triumph Books, 601 South LaSalle Street, Suite 500,
Chicago, Ilinois 60605

ISBN 1-57243-623-9

Design by Graham Webb
Design Principals, Warminster, England

Printed and bound in Singapore by
Tien Wah Press (Pte) Ltd

 Now in its third edition, *The Illustrated Golf Rules Dictionary* is well established as the standard reference book on the rules of golf and related decisions amongst amateur golfers of all abilities throughout the world.

My continuing thanks to the many rules experts around the world who have scrutinised the book and also to everyone who has written with comments and suggestions. As far as possible these have been incorporated, along with all the rules changes and new decisions recently introduced by the R & A/USGA, whom I would like to thank for their help in my attempt to promote a wider knowledge of the rules amongst the golfers of the world.

Finally, don't forget that it is a rule of golf that a player is responsible for knowing the rules (R6.1). Enjoy your golf!

Hadyn Rutter

The R & A/USGA have updated the rules effective 1st January 2004, and all the substantive changes are included in this book. For those already familiar with the rules, the changes of note for amateur golfers are as follows :

1. Guidance on etiquette has been expanded and for the first time the penalty of disqualification has been introduced for serious breaches of etiquette.

2. Turf faces of bunkers are not part of the bunker whether they are grassed or earth.

3. One of the definitions of a lost ball has been amended by providing that it is lost when a player has made a stroke at a substituted ball, as opposed to the old definition of 'when he has put another ball in play'.

4. A tee may not be longer than 4 inches – and you will be disqualified for using a nonconforming tee!!

5. A player can now remove loose impediments on the green by any method, provided he does not press anything down. (Previously they could be removed only by picking up or brushing with hand or club.)

6. There is no longer an automatic penalty if when moving a loose impediment within 1 club length the ball also moves; there is now only a penalty if the player moves the ball or causes it to move when moving a loose impediment – but within any distance.

7. There is an additional relief from an immoveable obstruction in a bunker, allowing the player to take a 1 stroke penalty and drop outside the bunker.

8. The definition of 'the Rules' has been expanded to include not only the Rules themselves but also all the decisions of the R & A/USGA interpreting the rules and the conditions of the competition in which the player is taking part. Don't forget … **Rule 6.1** requires a player to know 'the Rules'!!

9. The limit for the value of prizes which can be won by an amateur golfer has been increased to £500/US$750 in any one tournament, plus a further £500/$750 in a hole-in-one competition in the same tournament.

In order to have a reasonable working knowledge of the rules of golf, you need to have read (and understood) *The Rules of Golf* and *Decisions on the Rules of Golf* – the official publications of the R & A/USGA that are the definitive publications on the rules.

In approximate terms they comprise over 500 pages of information about 34 Rules, 120 sections and 103 subsections plus over 4,000 decisions of the R & A/USGA clarifying those Rules, sections and subsections, not to mention the definitions, exceptions and appendices. For example, if you want to know what to do about your lost ball, for the complete picture you would have to consider the interpretation of 13 of the 34 Rules plus over 40 related decisions.

It is probably because of the number and complexity of the rules that the vast majority of amateur golfers unwittingly breach the rules of golf almost every time they play. When it is unclear how to proceed in a given situation, it is rare for an amateur golfer to be able to be certain that his understanding of the rules is correct.

Seldom will he have a copy of the Rules available and be able to refer quickly to the relevant authority to obtain the definitive answer. In competition, most will adopt the second ball rule and then debate the problem afterwards in the clubhouse. In social golf the players will agree on a rough approximation of the rule in accordance with what seems fair and reasonable in the circumstances.

It is probably true to say that in no other sport is there such widespread ignorance of the rules.

The Dictionary attempts to simplify this mass of information by collating relevant definitions, rules and decisions in an easy to use alphabetical form. So if your problem is a lost ball, simply look under **Lost ball (l10)** and you will find all the information relevant to the particular circumstances of your lost ball – the basic rule, relevant decisions and the appropriate procedures and penalties, all in a concise form.

It is intended for use on and off the course by golfers of all abilities.

1 If you are a novice or occasional golfer, you will need to know some of the more obscure technical terms used in the Rules. Please look them up – because their meanings are often not immediately obvious and understanding the Rules is impossible if you do not know the meanings of the terms!

The following are the main terms:

Abnormal ground conditions (a1)

Addressing the ball (a2)

Animals (a10) – important to know whether they are alive, dead or 'burrowing'

Area of intended swing (a11)

Artificial devices (a13)

Attending the flagstick (a14) – means holding it

Ball deflected (b8) – relates only to a moving ball

Ball moved (b18) – relates to a stationary ball

Casual water (c4)

Changing the ball (c5)

Claim (c7) – polite word for a dispute in match play

Dropping the ball (d16) – not the accidental version

Fellow competitor (f2) – the person you are playing against (stroke play)

Hazard (h5) – a bunker or water

Influencing the position or movement of the ball (i9) – doing something you shouldn't

Lateral water hazard (l1)

Lie (l3) – where the ball has come to rest

Line of play (l7) – where you intend to hit the ball

Loose impediments (l9)

Stroke play/match play (s29) – important distinction

Opponent (m3) – the person you are playing against (match play)

Outside agency
Provisional (p16)/second ball (s3) – know the difference!
Rub of the green (r8) – nothing to do with touching or with the putting green!
Through the green (t10) – does not include the putting green
Wrong ball (w7) – not as obvious as you may think!

2️⃣ Simply identify the key words in the problem for which you want an answer and look it up in its alphabetical order, e.g. **Lost ball (l10)**.

But remember, your problem may have several different components, e.g. if with a practice swing you accidentally hit the ball, you need to consider whether it was a practice swing **(p12)** or a practice stroke **(p11)**. If it is the former, although you may not be penalised under the rule relating to practice swings, you will be penalised for causing a stationary ball to move **(b18)**!

3️⃣ To make this book as concise as possible and to enable you to refer to the more comprehensive information contained in *The Rules of Golf* and *Decisions on the Rules of Golf,* a few abbreviations have been used – for example:

- R12.1 – refers to a RULE as published in *The Rules of Golf*

- D12.1/7 refers to a DECISION relating to Rule 12 as published in *Decisions on the Rules of Golf*

- EQ is a point of golfing ETIQUETTE

- DF refers to the DEFINITIONS given in *The Rules of Golf*

4 One or two further explanations are necessary!

- The format of the entries given under the subheading **Basic Rule** are what the author considers to be the basic rule applicable to an entry. This is not necessarily the exact rule as published in *The Rules of Golf* as it may incorporate interpretations relevant to the rule as decided by the R & A/USGA and published in *Decisions on the Rules of Golf*.

- Likewise items under the **Procedure** sections are a combination of both rules and decisions presented as a practical guide as to what you can, cannot or should do in the particular situation.

- You will find littered throughout the text a selection of circled lowercase letters, e.g. (a). These are a summary of decisions relevant to the particular item against which the notation is made.

- In the **Penalty** section of each entry you will see that the most common penalty is *loss of hole/2 strokes*. Loss of the hole is the applicable penalty if you are playing match play; 2 strokes is the applicable penalty if you are playing stroke play.

5 A plea for forgiveness from the lady golfers! The masculine gender has been used throughout this book, but references to 'he, him and his' are of course deemed to include 'she and her'.

6 The Dictionary is intended for amateur golfers – professional golfers are often subject to additional or different rules imposed by the relevant tournament committee.

Acknowledgement

The Dictionary is of necessity a digest of the rules of golf and decisions relating to the rules of golf as interpreted by the author. It does not carry the official approval of the R & A/USGA, who do not therefore warrant the accuracy of such interpretations. Readers should refer to the full text of the rules and decisions as published in the official publications *The Rules of Golf* and *Decisions on the Rules of Golf,* which are published by the R & A/USGA.

The rules of golf are those in force and published as of 1st January 2004.

About the author

As an international commercial lawyer and professional organiser of golf tournaments, Hadyn Rutter has combined his considerable and unique experience of interpreting rules and regulations with a practical knowledge of the rules and procedural problems encountered by a keen but average golfer well used to being out of bounds, in bunkers, water hazards, lateral water hazards and the like.

The result is *The Golf Rules Dictionary* – written initially as a personal, easy reference manual for the author's own benefit because there were too many rules to remember and, even as a lawyer, he found difficulty in understanding some of the rules of golf!

The idea for publication of the book came from the realisation that the majority of golfers had the same problem!

a

ABNORMAL GROUND CONDITIONS

What is it?

Abnormal Ground Conditions (AGC) is the collective term for the problems encountered in the conditions known as casual water, ground under repair and holes, (a) casts (b) and runways (c) made by burrowing animals

(a) hole
• **no penalty** for lifting a ball to determine if the hole is that of a burrowing animal – the player must first advise an opponent/fellow competitor and give him chance to observe *(D25/21)*

(b) cast
• molehill is a cast if in its natural state but once flattened e.g. by a greenkeeper it becomes part of the course and there is no relief even if soil remains *(D25/23)*
• if a player elects not to take relief from a molehill in a bunker and subsequently touches it with his club during backswing he is deemed to have grounded his club – **loss of hole/2 stroke penalty** for touching the ground in the hazard – see **Bunker (b33)** *(D13.4/5)*

(c) runway
• does not include footprints *(D25/19.5)*

What is it? – burrowing animal

a burrowing animal is only one which makes a hole for shelter and habitation e.g. rabbit/mole/salamander/ground hog/gopher/crawfish – not dogs etc

What is it? – casual water

any temporary accumulation of water on the course (other than a water hazard) visible before or after (a) the player takes his stance (DF)

it includes:

snow and ice

overflow from a water hazard if outside the hazard (D25/2)

a pitch mark filled with water (D25/3)

it does not include:

soft mushy ground (D25/1)

water which appears when pressing a footmark down (D25/4)

dew and frost

manufactured ice

water on the putting green which was not visible when taking stance but which became visible when approaching the ball D25/5)

(a) **after**
• when water comes to the surface as a result of normal pressure from the player's feet in taking his stance

The player may lift the ball to determine if the hole is that of a burrowing animal

What is it?

Basic rule

Penalty

Exceptions

What is it? – Ground Under Repair (GUR)

any part of the course so marked or declared by the Committee. Stakes and lines defining it are within the GUR. The margin extends vertically downwards but not upwards (DF)

it includes:

- material piled for removal
- a hole made by a greenkeeper including stake holes even if not marked
- a fallen tree being cut up for removal (D25/7)
- pine needles piled for removal (D25.1b/17)
- a hole where stake has been removed from a water hazard (the hole is deemed within the hazard (D25/18))
- environmentally sensitive areas if so designated
- a tree, bush or other growing thing rooted in GUR (D25/10)

it does not include:

(unless specifically declared GUR by the Committee)
- grass cuttings left on the course and not intended to be removed
- a tree stump (D25/8)
- a fallen tree attached to its stump (D25/9)
- cracks in the ground (D25/12)
- aeration holes made by greenkeeper (D25/15) – see **Aeration holes (a5)**
- an old hole on the green which has sunk (D25/17)
- a rut made by a tractor (D25/16)
- a bunker being renovated (D25/13)

What is it?

Basic rules

1 the player is entitled to relief when his ball lies in or touches an AGC or when it is on the course and interferes (a) with his stance or area of intended swing or (on the putting green) his line of putt (R25.1a) – see Procedure

2 if a ball is lost in AGC – see *Lost ball* (l10)

3 when searching for a ball in AGC – **no penalty** if the ball is accidentally moved; the ball to be replaced in the player's estimate of its original location unless the player opts to take relief as per Procedure **2** (R12.1)

(a) **interference**
• if interference is from inside the GUR but the ball is outside e.g. long grass or branches growing inside interfere with a swing at the ball which is outside – the player is entitled to relief (D25.1a/1)

Exceptions

Penalty

Procedure

Exceptions

relief is not available if:

1. the hole is made by a non burrowing animal e.g. a dog – but the Committee may declare such holes to be ground under repair (D25/20) and relief will then be available (D33.8/2.5)

2. it is unreasonable to play a stroke because of anything other than the AGC (e.g. if a tree is in the way but stance is also affected by a molehill) (D25.1b/19 and 21) or

3. interference by the AGC would only occur because the player uses an unnecessarily abnormal stance, swing or direction of play (D25.1b/22)

4. the Committee has made a local rule denying relief from interference with stance by the particular AGC

5. a player may not brush away casual water – this is deemed improving the *Line of play* (see (l7)) – **loss of hole/2 stroke penalty**

Penalty

for breach of the relevant rules – **loss of hole/2 strokes**

What is it?

Basic rules

18

Procedure

the player may either:

1 play the ball as it lies (unless the committee has made relief mandatory by a local rule) **or**

2 take relief (a) by identifying and marking the nearest point of relief being the point on the course (b) nearest to where the ball lies which avoids interference by the AGC, is not in a hazard or on a putting green and is not nearer the hole then lifting and dropping his ball as follows:

(i) *through the green* – **without penalty** within one club length (c) of that point (R25.1b(i))

(ii) *on the putting green* (d) – **without penalty** place at the nearest point of relief or if maximum relief is not available at the point affording maximum possible relief as near as possible to the original spot (e) but not nearer the hole nor in a hazard (R25.1b(iii)) **even if off the green**

(iii) *in a bunker* (f) – either:
(1) – **without penalty** in the bunker as near as possible to the original spot but not nearer the hole and on ground which affords maximum relief from the AGC **or**
(2) – with **1 stroke penalty** (g) outside the bunker on the extension of the line between the original spot and the hole but not nearer the hole (R25.1b(ii) and c(ii))

3 relief without penalty is not available if the AGC is in a water hazard - the player must proceed under the rules re water hazards **(w2)**

Procedure

a — relief

• player may choose only one of the options for relief having chosen one he cannot then try the other if the first is unsatisfactory *(D25.1b/9)*

• if casual water is in GUR he may first take relief from water and then take further relief from the GUR *(D25.1b/11)*

• where the ball is in a tree growing in GUR but the ball itself is above a point outside the GUR, the nearest point of relief is still directly below the ball *(D25/10.5)*

b — nearest point on the course

• ball goes out of bounds but rolls into rabbit hole which takes it back in bounds – player may drop within one club length of the point vertically above where the ball came to rest *(D25.1b/23)*

• even if it means dropping into an unplayable position *(D25.1b/1)*

• even if the line of play is incidentally improved *(D25.1b/3)*

c — one club length

• the ball may then roll up to a further 2 club lengths – see **Club length (c11)**

• the player should measure with the club he intends to use for the next stroke - but he need not use that club for the next stroke may re-drop if he uses another club & the GUR still interferes with his stance/swing *(D20.2c/0.8)*

What is it?

Basic rule

Penalty

Exceptions

Procedure

d — on the green

• where the ball is off the green no relief merely because casual water on the green is on the line of putt – if the player brushes away casual water – **loss of hole/2 stroke penalty** *(D13.2/34)*

e — as near as possible

• if the best relief is off the green the player may place the ball off the green *(D25.1b/10)*

f bunker

• e.g. if in bunker completely covered by water (D25.1b/8) player can either drop in the shallowest water, adopt procedure 2 (iii)(2) or declare the ball unplayable.

g application of penalty

• if an entire bunker is GUR but classified as 'through the green' procedure **2**(i) applies – a player may adopt this option but **without penalty** (D25/13)

Hawaii

What is it?

the technical term for preparing to play a stroke at the ball.
The ball is deemed 'addressed' when:

1 the player has completed taking his stance **a** and

2 he is in the position from which he usually strikes the ball (D18.2b/4) and

3 he has grounded the club **b**

NB in a water hazard or bunker step ③ does not apply **c** and address is completed after ②

b **grounding the club**
• *a club is deemed grounded in long grass etc when it is sufficiently compressed to take the weight of the club (D18.2b/5)*
• *as part of the address procedure a player grounds his club in front of the ball before moving it behind – the ball is addressed when the club was first grounded (D18/5)*
• *if a player does not ground his club he cannot be penalised under R18.2b – but he may still incur a penalty under R18.2a – see **Ball moved – by player (b8)***

a completed taking his stance

• player addresses the ball then steps away – the ball moves when he is taking his stance the second time – **1 stroke penalty** as the first address counts (D18.2b/7)

• but when a player marked and lifted his ball on the green and it moved whilst taking his stance a second time – **no penalty** as the ball had been out of play and therefore the player was entitled to start the address procedure again (D18.2b/8)

• player stands behind the ball and aligns his putter then steps to the side and places his feet – he is deemed to have addressed it only when his feet are in the position from which he usually strikes the ball (D18/6)

C addressing the ball in a hazard

• ball in hazard moved after stance taken but before club grounded – the ball is addressed **1 stroke penalty** (D18.2b/2)

• in a hazard the player need not even have a club in his hand to be deemed to have addressed the ball if he takes his usual stance e.g. to get a 'feel' for the shot (D18.2b/2)

Basic rules

Procedures

Exceptions

Basic rules

1 on the teeing ground
(i) before, during and after address if the ball moves other than as a result of a stroke there will generally be **no penalty** (a) because the ball is not in play until the player makes a stroke at it (R11.3)

2 elsewhere on the course
(i) before or during address if the ball is moved by the player, his caddie, his partner or any of their equipment (other than as a result of a stroke) – **1 stroke penalty**
– see *Ball moved – by player (b18)* (R18.2a)
(ii) after a player has addressed it, if a ball in play moves other than as a result of a stroke – **1 stroke penalty** – as it is deemed to have been moved by him whether or not he actually touched it (R18.2b)

a **ball in play**
• *ball accidentally knocked off the tee before address is completed – replace **without penalty** (R11.3)*
• *after a stroke was played and missed on tee, the ball was accidentally knocked off the tee – the ball is then in play – **1 stroke penalty** and replace it on the tee (D11.3/1) – if the ball is knocked off the tee as the result of a stroke the stroke counts and the ball must be played as it lies (D11.3/2)*

What is it?

Procedures

1. the ball must be replaced
   – see *Placing and
   replacing the ball* (p8)

2. other players should not
   talk, move or stand close
   to or directly behind the
   ball when a player is
   addressing it (EQ)

Players should not talk.........

Exceptions

there is **no penalty** if:

1. the ball is not in play

2. the ball moves as a result of a stroke which is not
   discontinued – the stroke counts and the ball should then
   be played as it lies

3. on the putting green the ball moves after address as a result
   of brushing an insect off it – see *Loose impediment* (l9) –
   replace the ball (D18.2c/2). This exception does not apply
   elsewhere on the course

4. the movement after address was when the ball was struck
   by another ball – replace the ball (D18.2b/11) – see *Ball
   moved* (b18)

5. a ball at rest in a water hazard moves after address but this
   is due to the current – play it as it lies (D14.6/1)

a3 ADHESIVE TAPE

see *Artificial devices* (a12) and *Club* (c9)

Ballybunion Old Course, Ireland

a4 ADVICE

What is it?

the Rules are concerned only with advice which could influence a player's method of play, his choice of club or his method of making a stroke

Basic rule

a player may not give advice to or ask for or receive advice  **(a)** from anyone during a stipulated round (R8.1)

a advice
- deliberately offering misleading information regarding club selection – **loss of hole/2 stroke penalty** (D8.1/9)
- demonstrating how to play a stroke – **loss of hole/2 stroke penalty** against a player giving the demonstration – **loss of hole/2 stroke penalty** against a player receiving demonstration only if he asked for it (D8.1/14)

Penalty

loss of hole/2 strokes **(b)**

b how the penalty is applied
- in match play singles as soon as advice is asked for the hole is lost whether or not the advice is given (D8.1/25)
- in four ball (AB v CD) if A asks C for advice and C gives it, A and C are **disqualified** from the hole but the penalties do not apply to their partners (D8.1/25)
- in stroke play the player asking for advice suffers the **2 stroke penalty** and if the other player gives advice he suffers the **same penalty** (D8.1/25)

Exceptions

a4   Advice

Exceptions

a player may **without penalty** give or receive:

1. advice from his own caddie (a)

2. advice from his partner or his caddie (b)

3. advice re rules (c)

4. in team competition the Committee may authorise each team to appoint and identify prior to him giving advice one person e.g. team captain/coach who may give advice to members of that team (d) (R8)

5. advice not relevant to the hole being played (e)

6. advice obtained by observation (f)

7. advice on matters of public information (g)

(a) **caddie**
- obtaining advice from a caddie who is also caddie for an opponent regarding opponent's club selection – **no penalty** (D8.1/12)
- if a player's caddie asks for or receives advice from another player, the player is penalised – **loss of hole/2 strokes** – even if he personally does not hear or receive the advice

What is it?

Basic rule

Penalty

(b) **partner**
- depending on format players on the same team may not be partners – e.g. where a team competition is scored on the lowest aggregate of individual scores team members are not partners (D8.1/22)

C rules
• suggesting a player declares his ball unplayable is advice on method of play, not on Rules – **loss of hole/2 stroke penalty** *(D8.1/16)*

d authorised
• if the Committee has not authorised advice and advice is given by the captain there is **no penalty** under the Rules, but if the player allows this to continue, in equity he will be penalised **2 strokes/loss of hole** *(D8.1/24)*
• the captain may not give advice if he is playing in the competition *(D8/2)*

e the hole being played
• asking what club an opponent used at the previous hole is not seeking advice *(D8.1/6)*
• asking what club an opponent used at the present hole but after the player had played his stroke is not seeking advice *(D8.1/7)*
• advice may be given or received before or after, but not during, a round *(D8.1/18)*
• 36 hole competition is 2 stipulated rounds so advice can be given between rounds *(D8.1/19)*
• advice given whilst play suspended – **no penalty** *(D8.1/20)*

f observation
• looking into an opponent's bag to see which club is missing is not seeking advice *(D8.1/10)*
• but removing a towel in order to look into an opponent's bag to see which club is missing is seeking advice – **loss of hole/2 stroke penalty** *(D8.1/11)*

g public information
• includes length of hole, distance from permanent object (tree, bunker, sprinkler head) to another permanent object; position of flagstick, position of hazards (NB putting green and ball are not permanent objects) *(D8.1/1 and 2)*
• asking how far an opponent's ball is from the hole is not seeking advice *(D8.1/5)*
• asking how far his own ball is from the hole is seeking advice *(D8.1/2)* unless it is for the purpose of establishing distances to determine the order of play *(D8.1/2.5)*

a5 AERATION HOLES

What is it?

small holes made by the greenkeeper by artificial means in the fairways and putting greens of a golf course

Basic rule

there is no relief without penalty unless specifically provided by the local rules for the course (R33.8/App 1)

Penalty

for taking relief when not permitted – **loss of hole/2 strokes**
for breach of procedure – **1 stroke**

Procedures

if relief is permitted by the local rules:

1. a player may mark his ball, lift and clean it

2. through the green he may drop it – see *Dropping the ball* **(d16)**

3. on the green the ball must be placed as near as possible to the original spot but avoiding interference from the aeration hole/s

3. if a player wishes to lift his ball to see if it is on an aeration hole he must first announce his intention and then follow the normal lifting procedure (see **(l4)**). The ball may be cleaned even if elsewhere than on the green.

a6 AGREEMENT

Basic rule

players must not agree to exclude the operation of a rule or waive any penalty (R1.3)

a examples
• agreement to:
– concede short putts (D1.3/2)
– reduce 36 hole match to 18 holes (D1.3/7)
– miss out any holes during a match (D2.3/3)
– repair spike marks on line of putt (D1.3/3)
– tee off out of turn in match play (D1.3/1)
– waive the 14 club rule (D1.3/4)
– not to lift ball on the green (D22/6)
– knowingly record/attest a wrong score (D1.3/6)
– decide a match by the wrong form of play (D33.1/4)

Penalty

disqualification from the match/competition

b how the penalty is applied
• there is no time limit for imposition of the penalty – player was disqualified for breach of rule 3 days after match had been completed (R34.1a/1)
• but Committee has discretion to decide timing on imposition of the penalty in accordance with equity (D34.1b/8) by either
– cancelling the competition or
– applying the penalty only from the time of discovery or
– reinstating the player last eliminated by the offender or
– having all players eliminated by the offender play off
• and the Committee can decide to waive the disqualification penalty and substitute a lesser penalty (R33.7)

Exceptions

Exceptions

1. mutual failure to recognise a penalty situation is not an agreement under R1.3 (D1.3/5)

2. mutual failure to implement a Rule because of ignorance is not an agreement under R1.3 (D2.1/1)

3. an agreement to play out of turn in stroke play – **no penalty** unless done deliberately to secure an advantage. (D10.2c/2) **NB** in match play – both players **disqualified**. (D1.3/1)

4. an agreement in match play that a hole should be considered halved before play of the hole has been completed (D2.1/1.5) (c)

5. bona fide mistakes or rule oversights which do not constitute deliberate agreements between players (d)

(c) **without completing**
• if the agreement is made without playing any stroke at the hole – both are **disqualified** for failing to play a stipulated round (D2.1/1.5)

(d) **bona fide mistake**
• giving a handicap stroke at the wrong hole – **no penalty** (D6.2a/2)
• mistakenly playing a fourball match in foursome format – **no penalty and replay the match** (D6.1/1)

a7 AIR SHOT

What is it?

when a player intends to play
a stroke but misses the ball
completely

Basic rule

the miss counts as one stroke

Procedures

1 if on the teeing ground the
draught from the missed
stroke causes the ball to
fall off the tee, the stroke
counts and the ball must then be played as it lies

2 if the player replaces the ball on the tee he has illegally
caused the ball to move and incurs a **2 stroke/loss of hole
penalty** – see *Ball moved by player* (**b18**)

a8 ALBATROSS

a score of 3 under par for a hole – scores 5 points in Stableford
competition

a9 AMATEUR STATUS

What is it?

the opposite of professional i.e. the status of a person who plays golf as a non remunerative and non profit making sport

Basic rule

an amateur golfer must not receive remuneration in any form (a) as a result of his golfing skill or reputation or behave in any way detrimental to the best interests of the game of golf

(a) in any form
• in order to maintain his amateur status a golfer may not:
– receive payment or compensation for serving as a professional or assistant professional
– take any action for the purpose of becoming a professional
– permit his name or likeness to be used for reward in connection with his golfing skill for advertising or selling anything
– become a member of a professional golfers organisation
– play for prize money or equivalent
– receive payment for instruction
– receive prize money or vouchers for money
– convert a prize or voucher into money
– accept a gratuity in connection with a golfing event
– receive a reward directly or indirectly for a personal appearance related to his golf skill or reputation
– receive reward because of his golf skill or reputation for broadcasting/writing or allowing his name to be used for such when he is not the author
– accept expenses in money or kind to engage in golf competitions or exhibitions (except from family/legal guardian)
– accept a golf scholarship other than one approved by the R&A/USGA
– accept membership of a golf club other than for full payment
– undertake any conduct detrimental to the game of golf – including gambling

Penalty

Exceptions

Penalty

forfeiture of amateur status (a)

(a) **who applies the penalty**
• *enforcement of the rules of amateur status is undertaken by the R&A in Great Britain and Ireland, the USGA in the USA and the relevant National Union elsewhere*

Exceptions

an amateur golfer may receive remuneration as:

1 prizes of a symbolic nature appropriately marked

2 (i) prizes or vouchers (b) in any one tournament or event with a retail value of not more than £500/US $750

(ii) in addition he may receive further prizes or vouchers up to £500/US $750 for a hole-in-one competition in the tournament.

(iii) if he wins a prize in excess of £500/US $750 (e.g. a car) he may still retain his amateur status if he donates the prize to a well known charity without ever taking possession of it himself

(b) **vouchers**
• *may only be issue by the Committee for purchase of goods from a professionals shop or other retail source (they may not be for travel or hotel expenses, bar bill or club subscription)*

What is it?

Basic rule

③ reimbursement of actual expenses for attending functions other than golf tournaments/exhibitions in which the person is playing

④ a teacher/camp counsellor where less than 50% of his time relates to golf instruction

⑤ a writer/broadcaster where it is his primary career and golf instruction is not involved

⑥ a part time writer broadcasters where he is the author of the writing/commentary and golf instruction is not involved

⑦ a writer where golfing ability is not a major factor in the production or sale of the work

⑧ expenses relating to a golf tournament/exhibition where

(i) the player is training for or representing his country/ state/province/county/club/educational institution or

(ii) the invitation is unrelated to golfing skill or

(iii) it is exclusively a charity event or

(iv) the player is sponsored with the prior approval of his appropriate local or national body or

(v) the player is under 19 or

(vi) the player is representing an industrial/business golf team and within limits set by the R&A/USGA.

a10 ANIMALS

Preliminary

in certain circumstances the Rules give relief from problems caused by animals, birds, reptiles and insects but different rules apply to different animals:

1. dead animals – see **Loose impediments (l9)**

2. live animals moving the ball – see **Ball at rest – moved by outside agency (b18)**

3 insects – see **Loose impediments (l9)**

4 snakes and bees – see **Danger (d1)**

5 holes, casts or runways made by burrowing animals, birds or reptiles:
(i) ball lost in – see **Lost ball (l10)**
(ii) interference by – see **Abnormal Ground Conditions (a1)**

Emirates Hills GC Dubai

AREA OF STANCE OR INTENDED SWING

Basic rule

a player must not improve or allow to be improved his area of stance or intended swing by moving bending or breaking anything growing or fixed including immovable obstructions and objects defining out of bounds or by removing or pressing down sand loose soil replaced divots other cut turf placed in position or other irregularities of surface or removing dew, frost or water **(a)** (R13.2)

(a) **improve**
- *player removed crowd control rope to enable him to swing but this released a branch and impeded his area of intended swing; he replaced the rope and put branch back as before* – **loss of hole/2 stroke penalty** (D13.2/15.5)
  NB **no penalty** if done by outside agency
- *player removed and broke stake supporting young tree – immovable obstruction* – **loss of hole/2 stroke penalty** (D13.2/16)
  NB *he should have taken relief under R24.2b – see* **Obstruction (o3)**
- *player removed boundary stake interfering with his swing* – **loss of hole/2 stroke penalty** (D13.2/17) *even if he realised his mistake and replaced it before playing shot* (D13.2/25)
- *player bent back part of boundary fence* – **loss of hole/2 stroke penalty** (D13.2/18)
- *player moved fixed object outside course to improve area of swing* – **loss of hole/2 stroke penalty** (D13.2/19)
- *player knocked down leaves on practice swing – normally* **no penalty** (D13.2/22) – *see* **Leaves (l2)**
- *player shook tree to remove water on leaves – deemed improving area of intended swing* – **loss of hole/2 stroke penalty** (D13.2/23)
- *breaking off branch which interfered with backswing* – **loss of hole/2 stroke penalty** (D13.2/14) *even if during the backswing of a stroke which was discontinued* (D13.2/14.5)
- *player broke branch in area of intended swing but then decided to play out in different direction so used different area of swing* – **loss of hole/2 stroke penalty** (D13.2/24)
- *a player may probe for rocks etc. if he thinks his club may strike then provided he does not improve the area* (D13.2/27)
- *pitch marks made by someone else may not be repaired if they improve the area* (D13.2/21)

The player may not remove out of bounds posts...

...or bend (or have the caddie bend) tree branches

Penalty

loss of hole/2 strokes

Exceptions

41

Exceptions

1. **no penalty** if the player improves his area of intended swing
   (i) in fairly (a) taking his stance
   (ii) in making his stroke or the backward movement of his club for a stroke (b)
   (iii) on the teeing ground in creating or eliminating irregularities of surface
   (iv) on the putting green in removing sand or loose soil or repairing damage as permitted by R16
   (v) in grounding the club which may only be done lightly and not so as to press it against the ground (R13.2)

2. a player may **without penalty** move an object to the extent necessary to determine whether it is fixed or loose provided he returns it to its original position (D13.2/26)

3. a player may **without penalty** improve his area of intended swing incidental to taking relief under some other rule e.g. R25 when taking relief from abnormal ground conditions (R25.1b/3)
   – see **Burrowing animals (b34)**, **Ground under repair (g9)**, and **Casual water (c4)**
   or when it occurs incidentally to some other permitted action e.g. removing **Loose impediments** (see **(l9)**) (D13.2/34) or **Moveable obstructions** (see **(o3)**)

4. **no penalty** if the area of intended swing is improved by an outside agency (e.g. spectator/greenkeeper) provided the player did not assist in or consent to the improvement (D13.2/33)

Basic rule

5. a player may **without penalty** remove water hazard or lateral hazard stakes

a **fairly**
• includes (D13.2/1)
– backing into a branch if it is the only way to take stance.
– bending a branch in order to get under a tree
• but not
– deliberately moving branches out of the way
– standing on a branch to keep it out of the way
– hooking one branch behind another
– bending a branch to get a better stance when an alternative stance
could be used

b **stroke**
• branch broken in backswing; stroke aborted and then started
again – **penalty loss of hole/2 strokes –** because branch was
not broken in making a stroke

The player may remove water hazard posts and brush sand off the green

a12 ARTIFICIAL DEVICES

Basic rules

during a stipulated round a player must not use any artificial device or unusual equipment which might assist him in:

1 his play (a) or

2 making a stroke

3 gauging/measuring distance or conditions (b)

4 gripping the club (c)

(R14.3)

b measuring distance
• distance meter attached to golf cart – **disqualification** penalty (D14.3/1)
• compass is a prohibited device (D14.3/4)
• plumb line is an artificial device (D14.3/11) drinks bottle placed on green to gauge slope is (D14.3/12.5) but not a club used as a plumb line (D14.3/12)

a assisting play
• using a club to steady balance whilst playing with another club – **disqualification** penalty (D14.3/9)
• device on shaft which emits click if swing is correctly timed – **disqualification** penalty (D14.3/10)
• use of golf ball warmer – **disqualification** penalty – but not hand warmer (D14.3/13.5)
• use of golf ball with transmitter plus hand held receiver to locate ball – **disqualification** penalty (D14.3/14)
• use of video/instruction tape or the like during a round – **disqualification** penalty (D14.3/16)

c grip
• holding golf ball in hand against grip – **disqualification** penalty (D14.3/6)
• hand bandaged because of injury – player inserted thumb of other hand into bandage to assist grip – **disqualification** penalty (D14.3/7)
• taping fingers together to assist grip as opposed to being for medical reason – **disqualification** penalty (D14.3/8)

Procedure

players and manufacturers should in cases of doubt as to legitimacy
of items submit samples to the R&A/USGA for ruling (R14.3)

Penalty

disqualification (R14.3)

Exceptions

1. artificial limbs or special attachments to enable golfers with
   artificial limbs to play the game are permitted provided they
   do not give the player an undue advantage over other
   players (D14.3/15)

2. plain gloves/resin/towel/handkerchief applied
   to the grip of a club – provided this does not make it non
   conforming under R4.1c – see **Club (c9)** but not tape or
   gauze other than for repair or lead tape applied before a
   round to adjust the weight (D4.1/4)

3. distance markers on a course indicating distance to the green

4. yardage books/course
   planners (a) (D14.3/5) printed,
   written or electronic (D14.3/5.5)

5. standard spectacles or
   binoculars (D14.3/3)

a **course planners**
  • *committee may publish maps*
of putting greens showing the
position of the holes each day (D33.6)

45

a13 ASSISTANCE

What is it?

physical help or protection when making a stroke
– see **Advice (a4)**, **Artificial devices (a12)**, **Influencing (i9)**
and **Line of play (l7)**

Basic rule

a player must not accept physical assistance (a) or protection
(b) from the elements when making a stroke (R14.2)

> **(a) unfair assistance**
> • *assistance which is contrary to the spirit of
> the game results in disqualification e.g. – putting
> out to show a partner the line of his putt after the
> player's stroke has been conceded* (D2.4/6)
> • *deliberately putting away from the hole so that the
> next putt is on the line of a partner's putt and will
> show him the line* (D30.3f/6)

> **(b) protection**
> *e.g. caddie shielding
> player from the sun*
> (D14.2/3) *is not permitted*

Penalty

loss of hole/2 strokes

Exceptions

1 assistance prior to making the stroke **C**

2 a player protecting himself from the elements **d**

C **prior to making a stroke**
- *aligning the putter for his partner provided he moves away before the stroke is played* – **no penalty** *(D14.2/1)*
- *holding an umbrella over the player provided he moves away before the stroke is played* – **no penalty** *(D14.2/1)*

d **self help**
 • *a player holding his umbrella with one hand whilst playing a stroke with the other* – **no penalty** *(D14.2/2)*

47

a14 ATTENDING THE FLAGSTICK

What is it?

means holding the flagstick to demonstrate the position of the hole
or standing near enough to the hole to touch the flagstick (although
not actually touching it) whilst a stroke is being played

Basic rules

1. before making his stroke a player may have the flagstick
   attended, (a) removed or held up to show the position of
   the hole (b) (R17.1)

2. the ball must not strike the flagstick (c) or
   any part of the attender or
   the player's caddie or
   the player's partner's caddie or
   anything carried by any of them during attendance
   (R17.3 a and b)

3. if the flagstick is unattended and the ball strikes it the
   penalty only applies if the ball was played from the putting
   green (R17.3c)

Penalty

loss of hole/2 strokes against the player

NB – the attender may also be penalised – see (b)

a attending
• refusal to attend –
no remedy (D17.1/2)
• attender may be another
player, a marker or an
observer but a referee
should not attend (D17.1/3)
• attender may put a putter
in the hole to mark the
position and the putter
becomes the flagstick for
rules purposes (D17.3/6)

b how to attend
• attender may stand behind the hole i.e. on line of putt (D17.1/4)
• attender may remove flagstick and rest tip against the green behind
the hole – but this practice is discouraged to avoid damage to the
green (D17.1/4.5)
• attender fails to remove flagstick and ball hits it – if done
deliberately to prevent the ball going too far past – the player incurs
a **2 stroke penalty** under this rule and the attender under Rule 1.2
– see **Influencing the movement of the ball (i9)** – in match play
attender **loses the hole** as he incurred the penalty first (D17.3/2)
• if flagstick stuck in the hole or attender did not see the putt – **no
penalty** on attender but the player still incurs the penalty (D17.3/2)
• if done deliberately to cause a player to incur a penalty –
disqualified for deliberately influencing the movement of the ball
under R1.2 (D17.3/2) – see **Influencing (i9)**

c flagstick
• flag is deemed part of the flagstick
so if the ball hits the flag when attended
loss of hole/2 stroke penalty (D17.3/5)
• it is deemed impossible for
the ball to fall in the hole without touching
the flagstick if the flagstick is also in the
hole (D17.3/1)
• a putter inserted in the hole to mark its
position is deemed to be a flagstick for
rules purposes (D17.3/6)

Procedures

Exception

Procedures

1 the attender must remove the flagstick to allow the ball to drop into the hole

2 a ball which has struck the flagstick or its attender must be played as it lies

3 a player may not attend, remove or hold up the flagstick whilst an opponent/fellow competitor is making a stroke or whilst his ball is still in motion without his authority (a) (R17.2a)

4 the player himself may hold the flagstick whilst he taps the ball in but the ball must not strike the flagstick

What is it?

Basic rules

Penalty

Exception

unauthorised attendance  (a) – if a ball strikes the flagstick or any part of the attender during unauthorised attendance – **no penalty** against the player. In matchplay the attender loses the hole. In stroke play the ball must be played as it lies except if it was played from the green when it must be replayed (R17.2b) and the attender incurs a **2 stroke penalty**.

(a) **unauthorised attendance**
  • *flagstick attended by partner or caddie without player's authority – ball hits flagstick – **loss of hole/2 stroke penalty** as attendance by member of a player's side is deemed to be with his consent/knowledge (D17.3/4)*

Ailsa course, Turnberry, Scotland

b

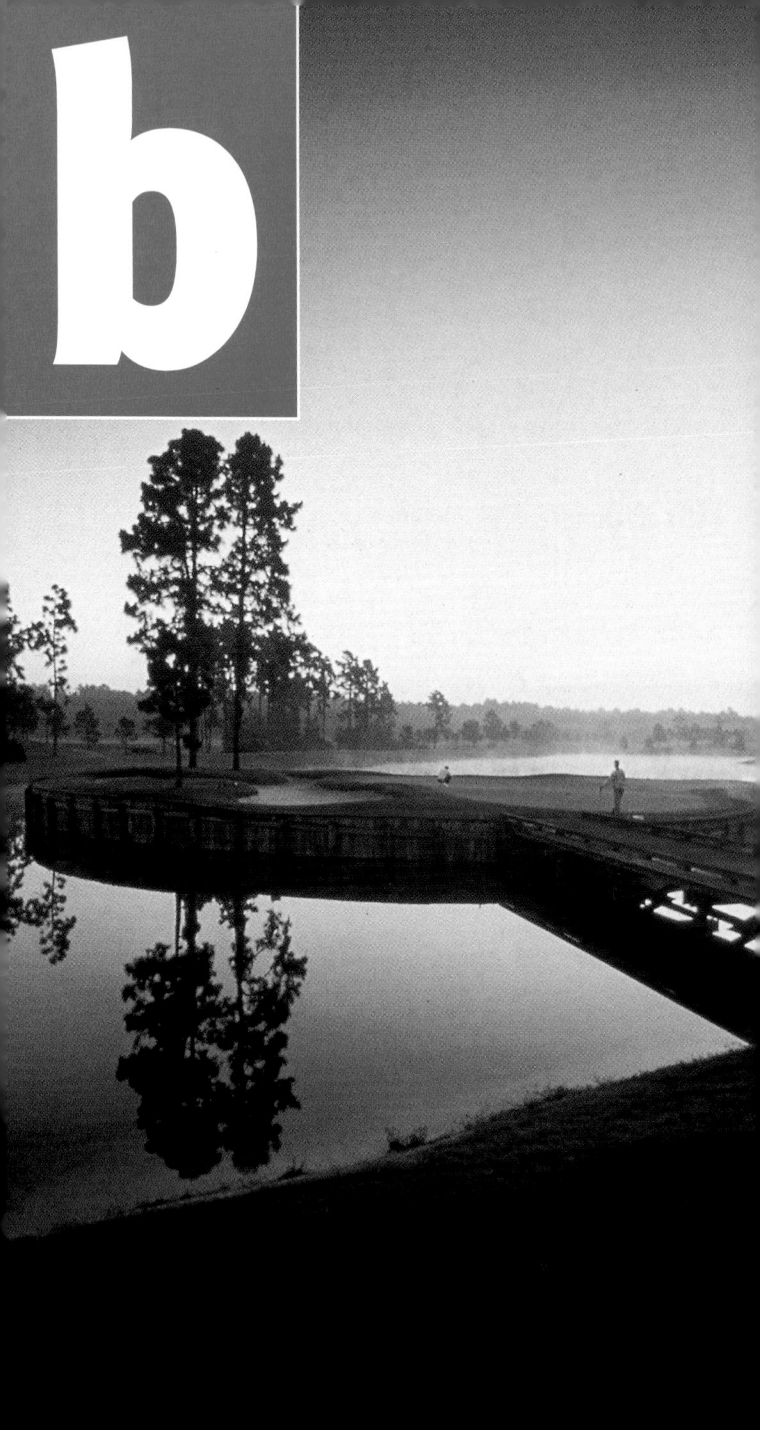

BALL – ABANDONED

see *Obstructions – moveable (o3)*
or if played – see *Wrong ball (w7)*

 # BALL ASSISTING PLAY

see *Ball interfering with play (b13)*

 # BALL – BROKEN

see *Ball unfit for play (b22)*

 # BALL CHANGED

see also *Balls exchanged (b10)* and *Substituting a ball (s31)*

Basic rules

1. during the play of a hole a player may not change his ball unless permitted by the rules – usually if it is either lost or unfit for play – if he does – **loss of hole/2 stroke penalty**

2. between the play of holes he may change his ball for any reason

Exception

1. the Committee may specify in the rules of a competition that only one type of ball may be used during the competition check the rules of the competition before starting the round

b5 BALL – CHARACTERISTICS OF

Main characteristics

- flight – it must not be designed manufactured or intentionally modified to have flight properties different from those of a symmetrically spherical ball
- size – not less than 1.680 inches (42.67mm) diameter
- weight – not more than 1.620 ounces (45.93 gms)

Basic rule

no foreign material may be applied to the ball for the purpose of changing its playing characteristics (R5.2)

Penalty

disqualification

b6 | BALL – CONFORMING

Basic rule

a list of golf balls conforming (a) to the characteristics set out in the rules is from time to time published by the R&A/USGA

Procedure

'X out' balls may be used unless it is a rule of the tournament that a conforming ball must be used *(D5.1/4)*

Penalty

for use (b) of non conforming ball – **disqualification** (c)

(a) conforming
• brands which have never been tested or which were previously approved but are not on a current list are deemed to conform unless the person alleging non conforming can prove otherwise *(DUS5.1/101) (applicable in USA only)*

(b) using
• non conforming provisional ball played but not counted, as original ball subsequently found – **no penalty** *(D5.1/3)*

(c) applying the penalty
• Committee may impose **loss of match/2 stroke penalties** instead of disqualification for use of non conforming ball *(D5.1/2)*

b7 | BALL – DAMAGED

see **Ball unfit for play (b22)**

Left: Le Chateau Montebello GC, Canada

Preliminary

the applicable rules and procedures vary according to whether the player's ball which was deflected (a) , stopped or moved was:

1 **stationary** – if so, see *Ball moved (b18)*

2 **moving as a result of a stroke** – if so different rules and procedures apply according to whether it was deflected or stopped:

(i)	by another ball	(page 52)

(ii)	by the player, his partner, either caddie or either of their equipment	(page 54)

(iii)	by an outside agency	(page 56)

(iv)	**Stroke play only** by a fellow competitor, his caddie or either of their equipment	(page 58)

(v)	**Match play only** by an opponent, his caddie or either of their equipment	(page 60)

a **deflected**
• *if the ball touches but does not deflect the other ball* – **no penalty** (D19.5/4)

Left: Vale do Lobo, GC Portugal

(i) by another ball

Basic rule

the player must play his ball as it lies (R19.5) if he moves it back to its original position – **1 stroke penalty** – see *Ball moved – by player* (b18(v))

Procedure

1. if the other ball was at rest it must be replaced **without penalty** (R18.5) – if not – **loss of hole/2 stroke penalty** (R18.5)

2. if the other ball was moving both balls must be played as they lie – if moved by either player – see *Ball moved* (b18)

Penalty

1. in stroke play only
   if both balls (b) were on the putting green and in play prior to the stroke (c) – **2 stroke penalty** (d) (R19.5)

2. if the player had played his stroke whilst another ball was moving after a stroke on the green – **loss of hole/2 stroke penalty** unless it was his turn to play (R16.1g)

> **b** **both balls on the green**
> • player putts and strikes a ball on the green from the group behind – **2 stroke penalty** (D19.5/2)
> • if player who has lifted his ball replaces it whilst other ball is in motion and other ball hits replaced ball- no penalty as both balls were not on green prior to stroke (D16.1b/3)

Preliminary

58

Exception

if his ball is stopped/deflected after a stroke on the putting green by a moving or animate outside agency ⓐ – the stroke must be replayed from its original position (R19.1b)

ⓐ **outside agency**
• e.g. a ball which had been lifted (outside agency) – **no penalty** (D19.5/1.7)

Wild Coast GC, South Africa

ⓒ **in play**
• player lifts his ball and sets it aside on another part of the green – another player putts and hits the ball – **no penalty** against either player as the ball was not in play – the other ball must be played as it lies (D19.5/1)

ⓓ **application of the penalty**
• if a ball hits 2 other balls and all are on the putting green only one **penalty – 2 strokes** (D19.5/3)

(ii) by the player (a), his partner, either caddie (b) or either of their equipment (c)

(a) **player**
• after a stroke the ball rolled back down hill and rested against a player's foot or club – when moved the ball rolled further – **penalty** and (stroke play only) replace the ball where it came to rest against his foot/club (D19.2/1)

Basic rule

if done either accidentally or deliberately the player is penalised (R19.2 and R1.2)

Procedure

1. in *stroke play* only – the ball must be played as it lies except

2. in *stroke play* only – if the ball lies in clothes or equipment it must be dropped (or on the putting green placed) as near as possible to where the article was when the ball came to rest (R19.2)

3. in *match play* – the hole is lost so there are no procedural consequences

b caddie

• *ball hit caddie and went out of bounds – **2 stroke penalty plus 1 stroke penalty** to get relief from OB under R27 (D19.2/2) (stroke play)*
• *ball hit player's caddie standing out of bounds and came back into play – **2 stroke penalty** and play as it lies (D19.2/3) (stroke play)*

c equipment

• *by golf cart – shared cart is deemed equipment of the player whose ball is involved – player penalised (D19/1) unless it is being driven by an opponent/fellow competitor or their caddie – **no penalty** and ball to be played as it lies or replayed from the original point*
• *if not shared it is always the player's equipment irrespective of who pulls/drives it (D19.2/6) unless the player was unaware it was being pulled/driven by his opponent/fellow competitor – **no penalty** and play the ball as it lies*

Penalty

if done accidentally – **loss of hole/2 strokes**
if done deliberately – **disqualification** (R1.2)

Exceptions

1 if a ball is dropped in accordance with the Rules and it strikes the player/caddie/equipment before or after it lands it may be redropped **without penalty** (R20.2a)

2 if the ball is deflected or stopped by a shared golf cart (c) when it is being driven/pulled by an opponent or fellow competitor – **no penalty** and the ball can either be played as it lies or replayed from the original spot (D19.1)

(iii) by an outside agency

What is it?

anything which is not part of the match e.g. a referee, marker, spectator, another player who is not part of the match (a), a caddie, a ball which is not in play (b), marker post, maintenance vehicle, power line (c) live animal (**NB** not wind or water) (DF)

a another player
• if taking part in a competition/match the other player on the course may be subject to **disqualification** under R1.2 for influencing the movement/position of the ball

b ball in play
• a players moving ball struck another ball on the green which had been lifted and put out of the way (outside agency) – **no penalty** (D19.5/1)

c power line
• the Committee may make a local rule requiring the ball to be replayed if it hits a power line (D33.8/13)

Basic rules

1 if done deliberately a decision must be made as to what is equitable (d) in the circumstances (R1.4)

2 if done accidentally it is deemed **Rub of the green (r8)** and the player must play his ball as it lies (R19.1)

d equitable
• spectator deliberately stopped putt on the green – stroke to be cancelled, replaced and replayed – **no penalty** (D19.1/4)
• spectator deliberately stopped putt running off back of green – the ball should be dropped where it probably would have come to rest (D19.1/4)

Exceptions

1 if after a stroke made other than on the putting green a moving ball comes to rest in or on any moving or animate outside agency **(e)** through the green or in a hazard the player must drop (or on putting green place) his ball as near as possible to where it came to rest in or on the outside agency

2 if after a stroke made on the putting green his moving ball is deflected by, stopped by or comes to rest in or on any moving or animate outside agency **(e)** except a worm or insect the player must cancel his stroke and, **without penalty** replace his ball and replay it (R19.1)

(e) **moving or animate outside agency**
 • dog deflected moving ball on green – stroke played from off the green – play as it lies (D19.1/6)
• ball from another group (outside agency) deflects moving ball after stroke on putting green – stroke cancelled and ball to be replaced (19.1/10)
• dog deflected moving ball on green – stroke played from on green – ball to be replaced as near as possible to original spot (D19.1/7)
• dog picked up ball on green and dropped it elsewhere – ball to be replaced as near as possible to original spot (D19.1/6)
• ball struck by knob on flagstick which came off when flagstick was attended – once it was detached it became an outside agency so stroke cancelled and replayed (D17/9)

Penalty

none provided the player follows the procedures above **but**
– failure to replace the ball – **loss of hole/2 strokes**
– failure to replace and replay after his ball is deflected on the green
– **2 stroke penalty** for playing from a wrong place (see **(w9)**) but if the breach was deemed serious the player is **disqualified** (D19.1/3)

Stroke play only

(iv) **by a fellow competitor, his caddie or either of their equipment** (a)

a **equipment**
• by golf cart – shared cart is deemed equipment of the player whose ball is involved – player penalised (D19/1) unless it is being driven by opponent/fellow competitor or their caddie – **no penalty** and ball to be played as it lies
• if not shared it is always the player's equipment irrespective of who pulls/drives it (D19.2/6)

Basic rules

1 if done deliberately a decision must be made as to what is equitable (b) in the circumstances (R1.4)

2 if done accidentally it is deemed **Rub of the green** (see **(r8)**) and the player must play his ball as it lies (R19.1)

b **equitable**
• fellow competitor deliberately stopped putt on green – stroke to be cancelled, replaced and replayed – **no penalty**; fellow competitor **disqualified** (D19.1/5)

Penalty

(C) none

C application of penalty
- if the ball, having struck a fellow competitor, subsequently also strikes the player he incurs a **2 stroke penalty** and must play it as it lies (D19.3/3)

d application of penalty
- when the fellow competitor deflected the ball into the hole and the player did not replace it – player **disqualified** under R3.2 for failing to hole out (D19.1/3) – see **Holed out (h7)**

Procedure

the ball must be played as it lies

Exceptions to Procedure

① if after a stroke made other than on the putting green his moving ball comes to rest on a fellow competitor or his caddie or in or on their equipment the player must drop (or on the putting green place) his ball as near as possible to where it came to rest – if not – **loss of hole/2 stroke penalty**

② if after a stroke made on the putting green his moving ball is deflected by, stopped by or comes to rest on a fellow competitor, his caddie or in or on their equipment, he must replace his ball and replay it from its original position (R19.1) – if not – **loss of hole/2 stroke penalty** (d)

Match play only

(v) by an opponent ⓐ , his caddie or either of their equipment ⓑ

Basic rules

❶ if done deliberately – the opponent suffers **loss of hole penalty and possible disqualification** for a serious breach under R1.2 for *Influencing the position or movement of the ball* (see **(i9)**)

❷ if done accidentally – **no penalty** (R19.3)

Procedure

either:

❶ play the ball as it lies ⓒ **or**

❷ before another stroke is played by either side cancel the stroke and **without penalty** replay it as near as possible from the spot where it was originally played

ⓒ **as it lies**
• *this option is not available if the ball, having been stopped or deflected by an opponent also subsequently strikes the player, his caddie or equipment (D19.3/3) he must replay the stroke* **without penalty** *– if he does then play it as it lies – **loss of hole penalty***

a accidentally striking an opponent
   • the ball strikes an opponent and goes out of bounds –
no penalty and replay stroke *(D19.3/1)*
 • during drop procedure ball strikes opponent – **no penalty**
and either redrop or play as it lies *(D19.3/2)*

b equipment
   • by golf cart – shared cart is deemed equipment of the player
whose ball is involved – player **penalised** *(D19/1)* unless it is being
driven by opponent/fellow competitor or their caddie – **no penalty**
and ball to be played as it lies or replayed from the original spot
 • if not shared it is always player's equipment irrespective of who
pulls/drives it *(D19.2/6)* unless the player was unaware it was being
pulled by his opponent in which case **no penalty** and ball to be
played as it lies
 • ball deflected by player's own clubs being carried in his opponent's
bag – **penalty** as they were the player's equipment *(D19.2/5)*
 • ball which has been lifted is equipment *(D19.5/1)*

Exception

if the ball lies in his
clothes or equipment
it must be dropped
(or on the putting
green placed)
without penalty as
near as possible to
where the article
was when the ball
came to rest *(R19.2)*

*The player may take
relief...... there is no
need to play it as it lies*

67

What is it?

the technical term for a plugged ball. The rules vary according to where the ball is embedded

(i) through the green

Basic rules

1 a ball embedded (a) in its own pitch mark (b) in a closely mown (c) area of the course through the green may be lifted cleaned and dropped (d) **without penalty** as near as possible to the original spot but not nearer the hole (R25.2)

2 there is no relief if embedded elsewhere through the green

3 the pitch mark may not be repaired until after the stroke has been played as this would be considered improving the **Area of intended swing (a11)** or area of drop (R13.2/10)

a embedded
- *deemed embedded even if it spins back into its pitch mark* (D25.2/1)
- *player may lift ball to determine if it is embedded but must first announce his intention to an opponent/fellow competitor – if not embedded it must be replaced* (D25.2/7)
- *it is deemed embedded in the part of the course where it entered the ground – if embedded in the face of bunker it is deemed in the bunker even though it may be beneath an area which is not bunker* (D13/4)
- *to be embedded at least part of the ball must be below ground level but does not necessarily have to touch the soil* (D25.2/0.5)

b pitch mark
- *to be deemed a pitch mark the ball must have been airborne – mis-hitting the ball and knocking it into the ground does not qualify for this relief* (D25.2/6)

c closely mown area
- *includes paths through rough cut to fairway height*
- *in thickly cut grass bank or in bunker – no relief* (D25.2/5)
- *does not include the turf face of a bunker* (D25.2/5)

d dropped
- *if embedded after redrop when taking a drop it should then be placed* (D25.2/2.5)
- *if it rolls back into the pitch mark when dropped – redrop it* (R25.2)
- *if having been dropped and played it rolls back into the pitch mark there is no relief* (D25.2/3)

(ii) on the green

Basic rule

the ball may be marked lifted and cleaned and the pitch mark repaired after which the ball must be replaced

(iii) in a bunker

Basic rule

the ball must be played as it lies or it may be declared unplayable and relief taken with **1 stroke penalty** as per Rule 28 – see **Ball unplayable (b23)**

(iv) in a water hazard

Basic rule

the ball must be played as it lies or relief may be taken with **1 stroke penalty** as per Rule 26.1 – see **Water hazard (w2)**

What is it?

BALL EXCHANGED

What is it?

when players inadvertently exchange (a) their balls during play
see also **Substituting the ball (s31)** and **Wrong ball (w7)**

a inadvertently exchanged
• balls on green marked and lifted by the same player but when replaced were inadvertently exchanged – players then putt with each other's ball – **2 stroke penalty** for both players – **loss of hole** for the first to putt in match play (D15.2/4)

Basic rule

a player must hole out with the ball he played from the teeing ground (R15.1)

Penalty

loss of hole/2 strokes (b)

b application of the penalty
• on the green a player lifts another player's ball by mistake and then replaces it where his own ball was and holes out with the wrong ball – as does the other player – the **player incurs the penalty** as does the other player who must also get correct ball off player and replay it from the correct spot – if not – **disqualified** (D15.1/2.5)

Exception ➤

Exception

no penalty if the balls were exchanged between holes  **C** or if otherwise permitted **d** by the rules e.g. when taking a drop, lost or unfit for play

C between holes
• balls inadvertently exchanged by players between holes so they hit each other's from the next tee – **no penalty** because by definition they are each playing the ball in play (D15.1/1)
• if it cannot be established when balls were exchanged it should be deemed to have happened between holes – **no penalty** (D15.1/2)

d otherwise permitted
• both players played ball into water hazard – caddie retrieved both but inadvertently exchanged balls – players each took a drop – error discovered on green – **no penalty** as R26.1b does not require a player to drop his original ball and substitution was therefore permissible for both players (D15.1/4)

b11 BALL HIT TWICE

see **Ball struck more than once (b21)**

Boulders GC, Arizona

Basic rules

1 a ball is in play from when a stroke is made at it on the teeing ground **(a)** until it is holed out, except when it is lost **(b)**, out of bounds, lifted or substituted **(c)** (DF)

2 when it has been lifted a ball again becomes a ball in play, when it is placed **(d)** or when having been dropped it touches an applicable part of the course – see *Dropping the ball (d16)*

a teeing ground

• *in stroke play the ball is not in play if played from a wrong teeing ground so strokes played and penalties incurred do not count – see **Teeing round (t4)** and **Wrong place (w9)***

b lost

• *ball believed lost but subsequently found in hole is the ball in play for score purposes even after search and playing provisional ball (D1.1/2 and 3) – see **Lost Ball (l10)***
• *ball believed lost and player drops another ball where the previous stroke was played – the second ball is in play even though no stroke has been made at it so if the original ball is then found the second ball is the ball in play and must be played. If original is played – see **Wrong ball (w7)***

c substituted

• *a provisional ball is not a ball in play if the original is found (D19.5/5)*
• *ball in play includes one substituted for the original ball whether or not this has been done properly in accordance with the Rules (DF)*

d placed

• *on the green it is in play when replaced and before any marker is removed (D20.4/1)*
• *it must be placed back on the correct spot; if not see **wrong place (w9)** if placed in a wrong place intentionally e.g to assess a putt, it is not in play*
• *if played in these circumstances it is a wrong ball see **w7** – **loss of hole/2 stroke penalty**.*

73

b13 BALL INTERFERING WITH PLAY

Basic rules

1. anywhere on the course a player may mark then lift his ball (a) if he thinks (b) that leaving it in play may assist another player (R22)

2. he may ask another player to lift a ball if he thinks it may interfere with his play or assist another player

3. a player may not insist that another player does not lift his ball (D22/6)

(a) **ball**
   • it must be a ball in play
   • an abandoned ball is an obstruction and may be moved **without penalty** (D24.1/2)
   • the same rules apply to a ball marker (D20/11)

(b) **thinks**
   • interference can be physical i.e. in the direct line of play or mental e.g. if it distracts the player's attention (D22/1)

Procedure

1 in stroke play a player may opt to play out of turn rather than lift his ball (D10.2b/1)

2 in match play if a player plays out of turn rather than lift his ball there is **no penalty** but he can be asked to replay the stroke in the correct order of play (D10.1c/2)

3 a ball lifted under this rule may not be cleaned unless it is on the putting green

Penalty

for failing to comply with the rules – **loss of hole/2 strokes**

C application of the penalty
  • if a player states he intends to move his ball as it may assist another player and that other player objects and plays before the ball can be lifted he can be **disqualified** for failing to comply with a rule (D3.4/1)
  • in fourball play if one partner is disqualified for failing to comply with the rule and his action assisted the other partner, he is also **disqualified** (D30.3f/11)

b14 BALL – LOST

see **Lost ball (l10)**

b15 BALL MARK

see **Pitch mark (p7)**

b16 BALL MARKER

What is it?

a small coin or similar item used to mark the position of the ball prior to lifting it when so permitted by the Rules

Basic rule

it is an outside agency and not equipment of a player, so if a ball is deflected by it the ball must be played as it lies – **no penalty** – see *Ball deflected by outside agency* (**b8**) also, *Marking the ball* (**m2**) for applicable rules and procedure and *Ball interfering with play* (**b13**) for rules if marker interferes with play

b17 BALL MISSED

when player attempts a stroke at it – see *Air shot* (**a6**)

a in play

- ball lifted and accidentally dropped hitting another player's ball – lifted ball is not in play and is equipment – **1 stroke penalty in match play – stroke play no penalty** (D18/7.5)
- ball moved by another ball after player has addressed it but before a stroke is played at it – **no penalty** and replace it even though the ball is in play (D18.2b/11)

b18 BALL MOVED WHEN STATIONARY

What is it?

when stationary and in play (a) a players ball leaves its position and comes to rest in any other place (DF)

Preliminary

where procedure requires a ball to be replaced, if it cannot easily be recovered it may be substituted

the applicable rules and procedures vary according to whether the player's ball which was deflected, stopped or moved was:

1 **moving** – if so, see *Ball deflected* (b8)

2 **stationary** – if so different rules and procedures apply

| (i) | by another ball | (page 72) |

| (ii) | by the wind | (page 73) |

| (iii) | **Match play only** by an opponent, his partner, their caddie or their equipment | (page 74) |

| (iv) | **Stroke play only** by a fellow competitor, his partner, their caddie or their equipment | (page 75) |

| (v) | by the player himself, his caddie or their equipment | (page 76) |

| (vi) | by an outside agency | (page 82) |

b18 Ball moved when stationary

(i) by another ball

Basic rule

it must be replaced (a) **without penalty** (R18.5)
– see **Placing/replacing the ball (p8)** for procedure

> **a** **replaced**
> • *it can only be replaced
> if the original position can
> be determined; if not it
> must be dropped – but
> placed on the green*

Penalty

for failure to replace the ball – **loss of hole/2 strokes**

Exception

another player's ball knocked away by a player hits his own ball –
as he is deemed to have caused his own ball to move **1 stroke
penalty** and ball to be replaced (D18.2a/18)

Preliminary

(ii) by the wind

Basic rule

a ball moved by the wind (a) cannot be replaced and must
be played from its new position (D18.1/12)

a **moved by the wind**
• ball oscillating on spot on green because
of wind is pressed down by the player to make
it stand still – he is deemed to have altered its
lie – **2 stroke penalty for moving the ball**
(D18.2a/6)

Penalty

loss of hole/2 strokes if the ball is replaced (R18)

Exceptions

1 ball lying on plastic bag (*outside agency*) is blown to a new
position by the wind – the ball should be dropped **without
penalty** at its original position as it is deemed to have been
moved by the bag not the wind (D18.1/7)

2 ball moved by wind/rain during suspension – the ball may
still be replaced **without penalty** under R33 which requires
play to be resumed from where it was discontinued
(D18.1/11) – see *Discontinuance of play* **(d6)**

Match play only

(iii) by an opponent, his partner, either of their caddies ⓐ or equipment

Basic rules

a ball may not be moved ⓑ or touched by any of the above after address and when it is in play otherwise than permitted by the Rules (R18.3)

Procedure

ball to be replaced if not – **loss of hole penalty**

Penalty

1 stroke penalty against the opponent (R18.3b)

Exceptions

① **no penalty** if it is moved in measuring to determine which ball is farther from the hole (R10.4)

② **no penalty** if it is moved during a search for a ball (R18.3)

③ **no penalty** if it is not in play

ⓐ **caddie**
• opponent's caddie accidentally steps on player's ball – **1 stroke penalty** against opponent and player's ball to be replaced (D18.3b/3)

ⓑ **moved**
• opponent disturbs bushes causing player's ball to move – **1 stroke penalty** against opponent and player's ball to be replaced (D18.3b/2)

What is it?

Preliminary

Stroke play only

(iv) by a fellow competitor, his partner, either of their caddies or their equipment

Basic rules

no penalty unless it is done with the player's consent (R18.2a)

Procedure

ball to be replaced – if not, **2 stroke penalty** (D18.4/1)

Chateau Whistler GC, Canada

(v) by the player (a), his partner, either of their caddies (b) or their equipment (c)

a by the player

• player placed his club in front of the ball as part of his address routine – ball moved – he is deemed to have addressed it – **1 stroke penalty** (D18/5)

• player placed fir cone against ball to stop in moving whilst he moved loose impediments – deemed touched by player – **1 stroke penalty** (D18.2a/32)

• player knocked ball from lip of hole in anger after he missed a putt – **1 stroke penalty** (D18.2a/23)

• player missed ball completely from tee shot – then lowers tee before playing again – **1 stroke penalty plus further 1 stroke penalty** for not replacing it (D18.2a/1)

• player missed ball completely from tee shot – then knocked the ball backwards in swinging the club after his stroke – **1 stroke penalty** (D18.2a/22)

• player presses down ball oscillating on spot on green because of wind to make it stand still – he is deemed also to have altered its lie – **2 stroke penalty** (D18.2a/6) – see **Lie of the ball (l3)**

Placing a fir cone against the ball to stop it from moving is not permitted

b by his caddie

• caddie lifted ball believing it to be unplayable – **1 stroke penalty** as caddie did not have authority to make decision and therefore moved ball illegally (D18.2a/15)

• caddie lifted ball for identification purposes without player's authority – **1 stroke penalty**

• **no additional penalty** for lifting without first announcing intention under R12.2 (D18.2a/14)

What is it?

Preliminary

a
• *player nudged his ball off the tee from his tee shot then put it back on the tee before playing again* – **1 stroke penalty for moving the ball plus 1 stroke** *for not replacing it* (D18.2a/2)
• *player dropped flagstick and moved ball* – **1 stroke penalty** – *unless done whilst measuring distances to determine order of play* (D18.2a/24)
  – *player throws rake in bunker and moves ball* – **1 stroke penalty** (D13.4/21)
  – *player climbs tree to play ball and ball is dislodged* – **1 stroke penalty** (D18.2a/26)
• *BUT if the purpose of climbing a tree is merely to identify the ball with the intention of declaring it unplayable and ball is dislodged* – **no penalty** *other than under the ball unplayable rule provided his intention was announced* (D18.2a/27)
• *IF the tree is shaken by the player believing his ball is in it – ball falls to ground* – **1 stroke penalty plus further 1 stroke penalty** *if the ball is not replaced in the tree* (D18.2a/28)
• *if a player is unable to replace his ball in the tree he should declare it unplayable* – **1 stroke penalty** (D18.2a/29) – *see* **Ball unplayable (b23)**

c **equipment**
• *moved by driver of golf cart (equipment)* – **1 stroke penalty** *against driver* (D18/8) *unless incident occurred during search for ball*

A towel is equipment

• *towel (equipment) dropped by player and blown on to ball which then moved* – **1 stroke penalty** (D18.2a/17)
• *hat blown off by wind moves ball* – **1 stroke penalty** *and replace ball*

Basic rule

Penalty

Procedure

Exceptions

(v) continued...

Basic rule

a ball may not be lifted, moved, caused to be moved (a) or touched after address and when it is in play by the player otherwise than permitted by the Rules (b) (R18.2a/b)

> (a) **caused to be moved**
> - *player is deemed to have caused ball to move if it does so after he has moved any loose impediment lying within one club length – only applies through the green (R18.2c)*
> - *if on the green – there is* **no penalty** *provided movement is directly attributable to the removal of a loose impediment*

Penalty

for breach of the rule – **1 stroke penalty** (c)

> (c) **application of the penalty**
> - *multiple breach of rule – i.e. dropping ball twice and then replacing it when it should have been replaced in the first place –* **only one 1 stroke penalty** *is applied, not multiple penalties (D18.2a/10)*

Procedure

the ball must be replaced; if not – **additional 1 stroke penalty** in *stroke play*; **loss of hole** in *match play*

What is it?

Preliminary

b not permitted by the rules

• dropped away from boundary stake in mistaken belief that entitled to relief – deemed to have moved ball and not replaced it – **1 stroke penalty for moving ball plus 1 stroke** for not replacing it (D18.2a/3)

• dropped instead of replaced – **1 stroke penalty for moving ball plus 1 stroke** for not replacing it (D18.2a/9)

• hit from tee into practice area and believing it to be out of bounds, lifted and dropped under R27 – then discovered practice area not out of bounds – **1 stroke penalty for moving ball in play plus 1 stroke** for not replacing it (D18.2a/11)

• ball accidentally trodden down by player in rough – lifts it and instead of placing it within 1 club length drops it within 2 clubs length – **1 stroke penalty for moving the ball plus 1 stroke** for not replacing it (D18.2a/21.3)

• played from ground under repair without taking relief – player then realised he could have taken relief, picked up ball and proceeded to take relief – **penalty for moving ball plus 1 stroke** for not replacing it (D18.2a/8)

• ball lifted in order to take relief from abnormal ground condition then player changed mind and elected to play ball as it lies – having lifted he could not change his mind and replacing was deemed moving the ball – **1 stroke penalty** (D18.2a/12)

• lifting a ball on the fringe believing it to be on the green – **1 stroke penalty** – but no additional penalty when the player also cleaned the ball (D18.2a/13)

Rotating the ball on the putting green to line makers name up to hole without marking or lifting ball – **1 stroke penalty** (D18.2a/33)
NB in photo ball has been marked – **no penalty**

Exceptions

(v) continued...

Exceptions

1. when the ball is not in play – **no penalty** (a)

2. if the player accidentally causes his ball to move it may be replaced **without penalty** in the following circumstances: (D18.2a)

(i) measuring to see which ball is farther from the hole (R18.6)
(ii) searching for a covered ball in a hazard/casual water/ground under repair
(iii) when repairing a hole plug or ball pitch mark under R16.1c
(iv) removing loose impediments (e.g. insect) on the putting green (D18.2c/2)

but a ball moved by the player's foot whilst moving loose impediments on the green – **incurs the 1 stroke penalty** (D18.2c/1)

What is it?

(v) when lifting/placing/replacing a ball under R20.1 and R20.3a (b) – see **(p8)** and **(L4)**

Preliminary

(vi) when removing moveable obstructions under R24.1 – see **(o3)**

Basic rule

(vii) with the club during address (c)
(viii) touching the ball accidentally through the green without moving it (D18.2a/31)

Procedure

(ix) repairing damage to the green (R16.1c)

Penalty

a in play
  • *practice swing moved ball off tee – ball is not in play* (D18.2a/19)
• *practice swing moved ball in play – **1 stroke penalty*** (D18.2a/20 and 30)
• *ball moved after stance taken but before club grounded – ball not addressed so **no penalty** unless the player caused the ball to move* (D18.2b/1)
• *BUT ball in hazard moved after stance taken but before club grounded – ball is addressed – **1 stroke penalty*** (D18.2b/2)

b lifting
  • *movement must be directly attributable to the act of lifting – accidentally kicking the ball when approaching to lift it – **1 stroke penalty** as this was not part of the act of lifting* (D20.1/13)

c address
  • *player placed his club in front of the ball as part of his address routine – ball moved – he was deemed to have addressed it – **1 stroke penalty*** (D18/5)

Waterville GC, Ireland

(vi)   by an outside agency ⓐ

ⓐ   **an outside agency**
    • *it is anything which is not part of the match (e.g. referee, marker, spectator, another player who is not part of the match, caddie, ball which is not in play, marker post, maintenance vehicle, power line, live animal BUT not wind or water) (DF)*
• *includes live snake; dead snake is loose impediment (D18/4)*
• *includes spectator – ball on edge of bunker rolled in when spectator walked past – (D18/10)*
• *and spectator who had been asked to attend flagstick (D18.1/10)*
• *includes stone dislodged when fellow competitor plays his stroke (D18.1/8)*
• *ball left in the middle of the fairway when play was suspended is missing when play was resumed – presumed moved by an outside agency – replace it as near as possible* **without penalty** *(D18.1/2)*
• *includes plastic bag – ball lying on plastic bag is blown to a new position by wind (not outside agency) – the ball is deemed moved by the bag and should be dropped (not placed) at its original position (D18.1/7) as the plastic bag was also a moveable obstruction – see* **Obstruction – moveable (o3)**

Basic rule

the ball must be replaced **without penalty** (R18.1)

Procedure

❶   for a ball to be treated as moved by an outside agency rather than lost there must be reasonable evidence to that effect ⓑ (D18.1/1)

What is it?

Preliminary

❷   the ball should be replaced not dropped even through the green

Penalty

for failure to replace the ball – **loss of hole/2 strokes**

Exceptions

1 a ball moved by an outside agency but not noticed by the player and played as it lies without replacing it – **no penalty** (D18.1/3) **NB** (C)

2 ball stolen by boy – player unable to determine where the ball had come to rest – player should drop the ball at a spot which is neither the most nor the least favourable area where it might have come to rest (D18.1/5)

3 ball moved by wind/rain or an outside agency during suspension – ball may still be replaced **without penalty** under R33 which requires play to be resumed from where it was discontinued (D18.1/11) (D18.1/2)

b **reasonable evidence**
• player treated ball as moved by outside agency without reasonable evidence – proper procedure was to have treated it as a lost ball; he was therefore playing from a wrong place – **loss of hole/2 stroke penalty plus further penalty stroke** for taking relief under the lost ball rules and the ball must be played from where the previous stroke was played if not – **penalty – disqualified** (D27.1/2.5)

C **not noticed**
• ball moved by outside agency but not noticed by the player who played it as it lies without replacing it – spectator points out that ball moved but player is not sure – player should play the original ball and also a second ball from the spot indicated by the spectator and then seek a Committee ruling – **no penalty** (D18.1/4)

89

Basic rules

when any part of the ball overhangs the lip of the hole the player is allowed a reasonable time to reach the hole plus 10 seconds (a) to see if the ball drops (b) (R16.2)

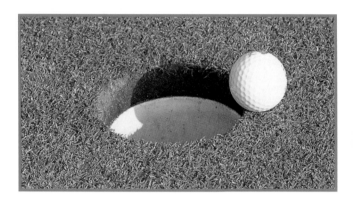

a 10 seconds
• player waited 40 seconds and ball then dropped – **1 stroke penalty** (D16.2/1)
• opponent conceded next shot after 5 seconds and knocked the ball away – **lost the hole** as the player was entitled to longer to see if the ball dropped (D16.2/2)
• opponent conceded next stroke then after time had elapsed ball fell in – **no penalty** because play of the hole was completed when the concession was made (D2.4/1)

b drops
• casting shadow on the ball to see if it will drop – **no penalty** (D16.2/3)
• jumping up and down to make the ball drop – **1 stroke penalty** under R18.2a for causing a ball to move when stationary – see (**b18**); or if the ball was moving **loss of hole/2 stroke penalty** under R1.2 for influencing the movement of the ball (D1.2/4) – see (**l9**)

Procedure

1. if the ball drops before this time – **no penalty**

2. if the ball drops after this time the player is still deemed to have holed out with his previous stroke – but must also add a **1 stroke penalty**

Exceptions

1. if the ball is lifted and replaced on the edge of the hole and rolls in when addressed – if it was not at rest before rolling in it should be replaced **without penalty** and then holed – (D20.3d/1)

   if it was at rest then **1 stroke penalty** as per ❷ above (C) – (D16.2/0.5)

2. ball overhanging the hole falls in after address – **1 stroke penalty** and the ball to be replaced as it was deemed moved by the player – see **Ball moved – by the player (b18)**

(C) at rest
• ball overhanging the hole was lifted and replaced – then fell into the hole – **1 stroke penalty** because it must have been at rest when replaced – if not it would have to be replaced again (D16.2/0.5)

Stamping to make the ball drop is not permitted

Basic rule

when the flagstick is in the hole and the ball is resting against it a player may **without penalty** move or remove (a) the flagstick or have it moved or removed to allow the ball to drop into the hole (R17.4)

(a) **allowing the ball to drop**

- *if in match play an opponent concedes the next stroke and picks up a players ball before the player has time to remove the flagstick and let the ball drop the player can replace the ball and allow it to drop – opponent **1 stroke penalty** under R18.3b for illegally moving a ball when stationary – see **Ball moved – by an opponent (b18)** (D17.4/2)*
- *in stroke play – ball to be replaced **without penalty** (R18.4)*

Procedure

1 if the ball does not fall into the hole it must be placed on the lip of the hole **without penalty** (R17.4) ; if it rolls away and is then played without being replaced – **loss of hole/2 stroke penalty** (D17.4/4)

2 if the player picks up the ball before it has dropped – illegal lifting under R20.1 – **1 stroke penalty** (b) and ball to be replaced against the flagstick (D17.4/1) – see **(L4)**

3 if another player removes the flagstick without authority and the ball rolls away
- in match play the opponent incurs **1 stroke penalty**
- in stroke play – **no penalty**
- in both cases the ball must be replaced and the player himself can then remove the flagstick and allow the ball to drop (D17.4/3)

(b) **application of penalty**
• *in fourball match play a player whose ball rested against the flagstick did not apply R17.4 and merely picked up the ball – the other 3 did the same believing the player had won the hole – should have been* **1 stroke penalty** *for lifting without marking under R20.1 and then* **disqualification** *for giving wrong information in not disclosing the penalty (R9.2) – partner also* **disqualified** *as player's breach had influenced the other side (D30.3f/3)*

BALL STRUCK MORE THAN ONCE

Basic rules

a ball may be struck only once  (a) by the club in the course of a stroke (b) (R14.4)

(a) struck once
• struck straight up in the air and landed on mud on the club face – no breach of R14.4 above but deemed to have been stopped by the player – breach of R19.2 – **loss of hole/2 stroke penalty** and ball to be dropped as near as possible to where it stuck to club (D14.4/1) – see **Ball deflected (b8)** **NB** D1.4/2 – allowed ball played from sand and stuck to club in similar circumstances to be dropped **without penalty**

(b) in the course of a stroke
• after a stroke the ball rebounded off a pipeline and struck the club – **no penalty** (D14.4/2) for multiple strike but **loss of hole/2 stroke penalty** as ball deemed stopped by player – see **(b8)**

Penalty

the stroke counts as one stroke but a **penalty stroke** must be added making a total of 2 strokes

Vilamoura II GC, Portugal

b22 BALL UNFIT FOR PLAY

What is it?

if it is visibly cut cracked or out of shape – not if merely scratched (a) scraped, paint damaged or discoloured, nor because mud or other materials are stuck to it (R5.3)

> ### a unfit
> • believed damaged internally because of erratic flight – no apparent external defect – no remedy (D5.3/1)
> • ball declared unfit and substituted then used at later hole – **no penalty** (D5.3/2)

Basic rule

if found unfit (b) the player may substitute another ball on the same spot (even in a bunker) (D5.3/5) **without penalty**

> ### b if found unfit
> • player may lift **without penalty** to determine if unfit if he has reason to believe so (R5.3)

Penalty

loss of hole/2 strokes for changing the ball when not justified

> **Procedure**

> **Penalty**

> **Exceptions**

b22 | Ball unfit for play

Procedure

1. the player must announce his intention to examine the ball

2. the ball must be marked and lifted

3. he must give an opponent/fellow competitor opportunity to examine it (a)

4. the ball must not be cleaned (b)

5. the substituted ball must be replaced on the same spot

6. if after inspection the ball is considered fit for play it must be replaced

7. if the player's opinion that the ball is unfit is challenged the matter should be referred to the Committee (D2.5/14)

Penalty

1 stroke for breach of procedure but this is not imposed if the player has already incurred the **loss of hole/2 stroke penalty** for breach of the rule

What is it?

Basic rule

Penalty

a **opportunity to examine**
• *player announces ball unfit but throws it into a lake before his opponent can inspect it –* **loss of hole/2 stroke penalty** *(D5.3/3.5)*
• *disputed claim – must be made before the player plays another ball (R5.3)*
• *unfit claim disputed but the player still played a substituted ball – the original ball was subsequently ruled fit when referred to the Committee –* **2 stroke penalty** *(D5.3/3)*
• *if condition of ball is disputed player should play second ball in stroke play and opponent should make claim in match play ; original ball should be preserved in disputed condition for inspection by committee (D5.3/8)*

b **must not be cleaned**
• *if ball is lifted under another rule which permits cleaning,* **no penalty** *if ball is also then declared unfit for play (D5.3/6)*

Exceptions

1 when a ball is broken in pieces as a result of a stroke **C** the stroke is cancelled and the substituted ball should be replayed as near as possible from where the original ball was last played

2 a ball may be substituted at any time and for any reason without the above procedure between the play of holes

C **as a result of a stroke**
• *broken because of impact with cart path deemed 'as result of a stroke' (D5.3/4)*

Cabo del Sol GC, Mexico

b23 BALL UNPLAYABLE

What is it?

a ball is unplayable if in the opinion of the player he cannot reasonably play a stroke at it because of its lie

Basic rule

a player (a) may declare his ball unplayable anywhere on the course except if it is in or touching a water hazard (R28)

(a) player
• caddie cannot declare a ball unplayable on behalf of a player – if he does so and picks up the ball – **1 stroke penalty** under R18.2 (D18.2a/15) – see **Ball moved (b18)**

Penalty

1 stroke and proceed as on page 100 **but** failure to adopt the correct procedure **loss of hole/2 stroke penalty**

Procedure ➤

Procedure

1 unless adopting procedure 3(i) the player must be able to identify his ball in order to declare it unplayable; if he cannot see it or identify it he must treat it as a lost ball and apply the lost ball rules

2 he must announce his intention to declare it unplayable then lift the ball – he may also clean it

3 having taken the **1 stroke penalty** he then has 3 options:

(i)	play a ball as near as possible from the spot where his original ball was last played (b)

or

(ii)	drop his ball within 2 club lengths of where it last lay (c) but not nearer the hole (d)

or

(iii)	drop his ball any distance behind the spot where his ball originally lay but on the extension of the line between that spot and the hole (d)

NB after declaring his ball unplayable a player may change his mind (e) as to which option he adopts even if he has put the ball into into play by dropping it (D28/13) unless he had dropped pursuant to a rule other than the ball unplayable rule – e.g. when dropping/redropping under R20/2a or R20/2c – see **Dropping (d16)** – in which case he cannot change his relief option (D20.6/2)

What is it?

Basic rule

Penalty

Procedure

b option (i)

• ball in deep canyon so the player cannot identify it – he may still declare it unplayable without identifying it, but cannot adopt options (ii) or (iii) because they require identification of the ball and access to the original spot (D28/1)

• player mistakenly declares stray ball unplayable and adopts option (i) – stray ball became ball in play and the original ball is deemed lost (D28/14) but if he adopted options (ii) or (iii) which require correct identification of the ball he would have played a wrong ball – **loss of hole/2 stroke penalty** and in stroke play he would have to continue with his original ball (D28/15)

• under option (i) if the player misses the ball and then declares it unplayable the miss is the spot where the ball was last played (D28/7)

• under option (i) if the spot where it was last played is nearer the hole a player may still invoke the option (D28/8)

c where it last lay

• if this is in a tree he may drop within 2 club lengths of the point on the ground vertically below its original position (D28/11)

• if the ball is at the base of a cliff he may not drop within 2 club lengths at the top of the cliff (D28/12)

d drop

• unplayable ball dropped into another unplayable position – the player must take a **further 1 stroke penalty** (D28/3)

• if the ball is in a bunker and the player adopts (ii) or (iii) the ball must be dropped in the bunker **NB** if it is on grass in the bunker he does not have to drop in the bunker as this is not part of the bunker (D28/9)

• if he drops outside the bunker and improves its lie substantially – **disqualified** – but if it is dropped in the same place as if he had adopted option (i) – **2 stroke penalty plus further 1 stroke** under option (i) (D28/10)

e change his mind

• player declared his ball unplayable and lifted it out of ground under repair – he then realised he could take relief from GUR **without penalty** – he may do so as he had not dropped a ball under the ball unplayable rule so it was not in play (D28/13)

Procedure

101

if the player has played his stroke from the 178 yard marker and the ball has gone through the green coming to rest against the wall:

Procedure option

❸ **(i)** is available and requires the player to return to the 178 yard marker and play again from the there with **1 stroke penalty**

❸ **(ii)** is also available with **1 stroke penalty** allowing him to drop within two club lengths of where the ball lay against the wall but not nearer the hole. The problem here is that the wall may still interfere

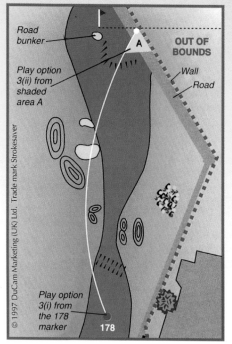

Road bunker

Play option 3(ii) from shaded area A

© 1997 DuCam Marketing (UK) Ltd. Trade mark Strokesaver

Play option 3(i) from the 178 marker

A

OUT OF BOUNDS

Wall
Road

178

with his new area of swing. Being a boundary wall it is not an immovable obstruction from which relief can be taken without further penalty – see **Obsructions (o3)**

❸ **(iii)** is not available as the extension of the line from the hole through where the ball lies against the wall is out of bounds

The Road Hole. 17th The Old Course, St. Andrews, Scotland

b24 BEST BALL

a form of match play in which one player plays against the better ball of 2 other players or the best ball of 3 other players (DF) for rules, procedures and interpretations see *Four ball match play* (f9)

b25 BETTER BALL

match play or stroke play game when two players each playing their own ball ('a side') score the better of their two scores at each hole against the 'better ball' of the other two (DF) for rules and procedures see *Four ball* (f9)

b26 BIRD

for rules, procedures and interpretations regarding holes casts and runways made by birds see *Animals* (a10)

b27 BIRDIE

the term used to denote a score of one stroke under par for a hole – scores 3 points in Stableford competition

b28 BIRD'S NEST

Basic rule

if a ball comes to rest in or near a bird's nest the player may **without penalty** drop the ball as near as possible to the original spot but not nearer the hole at a point which allows him to make a stroke without damaging the nest. If the ball is in a hazard it must be dropped in a hazard (D1.4/9)

TPC Scottsdale, Arizona

b29 BOGEY

the term used to denote a score of one stroke over par for a hole – scores 1 point in Stableford competition

b30 BOGEY COMPETITION

a form of stroke play competition in which play is against a fixed score at each hole – scored as in match play with the winner being the player who wins the most holes in aggregate (R32.1a)

b31 BRANCHES

- if attached to a tree/bush – see **Area of intended swing (a11)**
- if detached – see **Loose impediments (l9)**

b33 BUNKER

What is it?

a hazard which is usually hollow, consisting of a prepared area (a) from which the turf or soil has been removed and replaced with sand (b) or similar material (DF)

(a) prepared area
- *grass bordering or within a bunker is not part of it*
- *sand spilled over the margin of a bunker is not part of it*
- *margin extends vertically downwards but not upwards* (DF)
- *ball on the edge of a bunker overhanging it but not touching the sand is not in the bunker* (D13/3)
- *ball embedded in the vertical wall of a bunker is in the bunker i.e. is not deemed to have gone through the margin of the bunker so it cannot be declared unplayable and dropped outside the bunker* (D13/4)

- *ball lying on an obstruction in a bunker is deemed in the bunker* (D13/5)
- *earth wall of a bunker touched during backswing –* **loss of hole/2 stroke penalty** *as earth wall as opposed to artificial wall is not an obstruction* (D13.4/34)
- *mound made by burrowing animal in bunker interfered with backswing and was touched by a player in the course of making his stroke –* **loss of hole/2 stroke penalty** (D13.4/5)
- *tree in a bunker is not part of the bunker* (D13/2)
- *a staked turf face whether grassed or earth is not part of the bunker*

b sand

• spilled over the margin of a bunker is not part of the bunker (D13/1)

• knocked down from the side of a bunker to make a level stance is deemed building a stance – **loss of hole/2 stroke penalty** (D13.3/3)

• touched after a bunker shot but the ball then rolled back into the bunker – **no penalty** provided the ball was outside the bunker when the sand was touched (D13.4/35.5)

• smoothed after bunker shot which left the ball in the bunker – **no penalty** because this was not deemed testing the condition of the sand as this had already been done with the first shot and did not improve the lie of the ball or his stance (D13.4/36)

• smoothed after bunker shot which left the ball in the bunker – the player then discovered he had played out of turn and

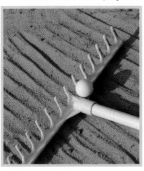

A ball on a rake in a bunker is deemed in the bunker

in match play was asked to replay his stroke – **loss of hole penalty** because it was presumed that smoothing the sand assisted the replay of the stroke (D13.4/39)

• smoothed after a bunker shot which put the ball out of bounds/lost and before a second ball was dropped in the bunker – **no penalty** because prohibitions only apply when the ball is in the hazard so he could also take practice swings and touch the sand (D13.4/37)

Basic rule

Exceptions

Penalty

Procedure

107

Basic rule ❶

before making a stroke at a ball lying in ⓒ a bunker or other hazard a player must not (R13.4)

(i) test the condition of the bunker or any similar hazard ⓓ

(ii) touch the ground in the bunker with a club or hand ⓓ

(iii) touch or move any **Loose impediment (l9)** in or touching the bunker

ⓒ lying in

• if the player lifts the ball e.g. having declared it unplayable – he may still not test the condition etc. as the ball must be dropped/placed back in the bunker (D13.4/35.7)

• but if he plays the ball from a bunker and subsequently has to drop it back in e.g. if it went out of bounds he is permitted to touch the sand etc. before the ball is dropped (D13.4/37)

What is it? *A player may not remove stones from a bunker unless authorised by a local rule*

d testing the condition

  • *touching the ground in a bunker during the course of a practice swing – is deemed testing the condition (D13.4/3) but touching casual water in the bunker is not (D13.4/7)*
- *hitting sand with a club in anger after failing to get out of a bunker – deemed testing the condition as a further stroke had still to be played from the bunker (D13.4/35)*
- *touching sand in a bunker with a club is permitted if the ball lies outside the bunker (D13.4/1)*
- *touching is not permitted even if it occurs otherwise than in preparing for a stroke e.g. leaning on a club whilst waiting to play a stroke (D13.4/2)*
- *touching sand during backswing – **loss of hole/2 stroke penalty** (D13.4/31)*
- *mound made by burrowing animal in a bunker interfered with backswing and was touched by the player in the course of making his stroke – **loss of hole/2 stroke penalty** (D13.4/5)*
- *'digging in' without having a club in hand in order to get a feel for the shot is not deemed testing the condition D13.4/24)*

- *taking a firm stance away from the ball and simulating a shot is deemed testing the condition – **loss of hole/2 stroke penalty** (D13.4/25)*
- *taking a firm stance then deciding to change the club is not deemed testing the condition – (D13.4/26)*
- *in foursomes the player played a bunker shot and having failed to get out then hit the sand in disgust – as his partner still had to play from the bunker this was deemed touching the ground in the hazard (see **Bunker (b33)**) and the side suffered the **loss of hole penalty** (D29/5)*
- *testing the condition of sand – nothing prohibits a player from testing the condition of a hazard provided his ball is not lying in or touching the hazard (D13.2/30)*

Exceptions

Basic rules

Penalty

Procedure

Exceptions to Basic rule ❶

❶ the player may touch the ground:
(i) as a result of or to prevent himself falling
(ii) in removing an obstruction
(iii) in measuring
(iv) in retrieving, lifting, placing or replacing a ball under the Rules
(v) he may place his clubs in the bunker **provided** nothing is done which constitutes testing the condition of the bunker or improving the lie of the ball
(vi) in probing for a ball believed to be in the bunker but covered with leaves (D12.1/4)

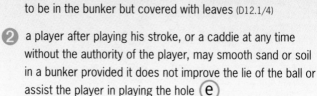

❷ a player after playing his stroke, or a caddie at any time without the authority of the player, may smooth sand or soil in a bunker provided it does not improve the lie of the ball or assist the player in playing the hole ⓔ

❸ if the lie of a player's ball is affected by something after it came to rest (e.g. a divot from another player's stroke) ⓕ the player may remove it **without penalty** as he is entitled to his original lie (D13.4/18)

❹ stones in bunkers are loose impediments and may not be touched or moved UNLESS in the local rules for the course they are declared to be **Moveable obstructions (o3)** and as such can be removed **without penalty** – check the local rules of the course (R33.8)

What is it?

Basic rule

A player may place her clubs in a bunker

e improve the lie
• if the ball subsequently returns to the bunker e.g. from his next stroke, he is not deemed to have improved his lie *(D13.4/38)*

f something
• **NB** – pine cone fell from tree and came to rest adjacent to a ball in a bunker – the player could not move it as *D13.4/18* only applies to acts of a player, caddie or other animate outside agency *(D13.4/18.5)*

Basic rule

Exceptions

Procedure

Penalty

Basic rule ❷

rules permitting lifting, cleaning and identifying the ball do not apply in a bunker (R12.2)

Exceptions to Basic rule ❷

when searching (see **(s4)**) for a ball in a bunker – if the ball is covered by loose impediments/sand the player may remove it by probing, raking or other means enough to see a part of the ball. If any excess is removed and/or the ball moved – **no penalty** – but the ball must be replaced and recovered so that only part is visible (**g**) (R12.1)

g **visible**
• *ball in hazard not visible at the address position but visible from another angle may not be further uncovered* (D12.1/3)

Procedure

❶ in a bunker the ball must be played as it lies unless the player chooses to declare it unplayable and proceeds under the *Ball unplayable* rules **(b23)**

❷ the player should fill up and smooth over holes and footprints made by him – but only after he has played his stroke (EQ) and the ball has come out of the bunker

What is it?

Basic rule

Exceptions

3 addressing the ball in a bunker – the club must not be grounded – taking stance alone is deemed addressing the ball **(h)** (DF)

4 dropping the ball in – see ***Dropping and redropping the ball* (d16)**

5 footprints in a bunker:

• made by a player searching for his buried ball may not be raked by him prior to playing a stroke when the ball is found – but may be raked by his caddie on his own initiative

provided the lie of the ball is not improved (D13.4/11)

• made by one player may be raked over after play at the request of another player who is also in the bunker (D13.4/19)

• made by a player whose ball is outside a bunker when he walks through the bunker to view his line to the green – then rakes out footprints before playing – **loss of hole/2 stroke penalty** because having worsened his line of play he cannot subsequently improve it (D13.2/29)

• ball in footprint must be played as it lies

(h) **addressing the ball**
• *ball accidentally touched but not moved when a player addressed it in a bunker –* **no penalty** (D13.4/12)

Procedure

Penalty

113

Procedure

6 rake:
- placed in bunker before playing a stroke – **no penalty** provided the lie of ball/line of play are not improved nor does it constitute testing (D13.4/20)
- sticking handle of rake in a bunker is deemed testing condition – (D13.4/22)
- thrown in bunker moves ball – **1 stroke penalty** and ball to be replaced (D13.4/21)
- used by member of greenkeeping staff whilst ball is in the bunker thus improving the lie – **no penalty** if not done on the instructions of the player (D13.2/4)
- used by a player when his ball is outside a bunker and the bunker is between his ball and the hole – deemed **Improving line of play** (D13.2/28) **(l7)**
- should be placed outside bunkers and in a position least likely to interfere with play (D misc 2)
- ball on or against rake – see **Obstructions – moveable (o3)**

7 water in – see **Casual water (c4)**

8 two balls lying closed together in a bunker – mark and lift the ball nearer the hole so that the farther ball can be played. Then replace the nearer ball without penalty recreating a lie as near as possible to the original e.g. if it was part buried it must be replaced part buried – see **Lie of the ball (l13)**

What is it?

Basic rule

Exceptions

Procedure

Penalty

for breach of the rules – **loss of hole/2 strokes**

Sticking the handle of the rake in the bunker is deemed testing its condition

b34 BURROWING ANIMAL

see *Abnormal Ground Conditions* (a1)

C

What is it?

is a person (a) who carries or handles a player's clubs (b) during play or otherwise assists (b) him in accordance with the Rules (DF)

(a) person
• *a caddie can be anyone unless restrictions are imposed by the Committee (D6.4/2)*
• *including a player who is not playing at the same time e.g. if he has withdrawn from the round or is playing later (D6.4/8 and 9)*
• *Committee may ban caddies from a competition or restrict a player's choice of caddies (R6.4)*

(b) assists
• *non player driving a cart or pulling a player's trolley is deemed to be a caddie (D6.4/2.5)*
• *person carrying an umbrella for a player is not a caddie (D6.4/5)*

Basic rules

1. the breach of a rule by a caddie is deemed the player's breach (R6.4)

2. there can be only one caddie per player (c) at any one time (R6.4)

3. a shared caddie (d) employed by more than one player is deemed to be the caddie of the player involved in a problem situation unless he is acting on the specific directions of another player (DF)

4. for rules where a ball is moved or deflected by a caddie – see **Ball moved (b18)** or **Ball deflected (b8)**

Procedures

Penalty

C **one**
- he may have more than one per round provided only one at any given time (D6.4/7)
- caddie may not have a person to assist him (D6.4/4) but casual temporary assistance e.g. 2nd caddie carries 2 bags whilst the first returns to pick up a dropped club is not a breach of rule (D6.4/4.5)

d **shared caddie**
- having handed a club to A the caddie places the bags of A and B behind the green and B's putt hits A's bag – *2 stroke penalty* to B because the caddie is deemed acting for B as A did not specifically instruct placing of the bags (D6.4/1)
- shared caddie pulls 2 carts – stroke by A hits B's cart – cart is considered A's for this purpose – *2 stroke penalty* to A (D6.4/6)

What is it?

Basic rules

Procedures

① for amateur golfers, caddies are only available for hire at a few major courses. The types of caddie range from someone simply to carry the golf bag to skilled golfers whose advice is invaluable as they know every inch of the course

② in addition to carrying the player's bag, driving a cart, pulling a trolley and providing general assistance he may, eventhough not instructed by the player (D6.4/10) search for the ball, repair old hole plugs and ball marks, clean the ball, remove loose impediments, mark the position of the ball and remove moveable obstructions

Penalty

loss of hole / 2 stroke penalty for each hole at which the breach occurred – **maximum 2 holes / 4 stroke penalty** ; for continuing to use more than one caddie after discovery of the breach – **disqualification**. (R6.4)

 CAR PARK

see *Obstruction – immoveable* **(o3)**

 CART PATH

see *Obstruction – immoveable* **(o3)**

C4 CASUAL WATER

see *Abnormal Ground Conditions* (a1)

C5 CHANGING THE BALL

see *Ball changed* (b4), *Ball exchanged* (b10), and *Substituting a ball* (s31)

Hyatt Grand Champions GC, California

CHILDREN/NON GOLFERS

see *Outside agencies* (o6) for rules purposes

What is it?

many golf clubs do not allow children/non golfers/golfers who are not actually playing to accompany players around the course because of the risk of injury – so it is advisable for players to check with the golf club in advance if they are contemplating having a non player accompany them other than as a caddie

What is it?

the term used in match play to denote a protest by a player regarding a possible breach of rule (a) by his opponent

(a)   possible breach
- *in match play a player may if he wishes overlook a Rules breach by his opponent provided there is no agreement between the players to waive the Rules (D2.5/1)*

Basic rules

1 if possible the dispute should be referred to the Committee

BUT

2 if a Committee member is not available within a reasonable time of the incident the players must continue the match without delay but the claim must be made by the player to his opponent before play is commenced from the next tee, **(b)** or if it relates to the final hole, before all players leave the putting green (R2.5)

(b)   before playing from the next tee
- *players mistakenly believe a match is all square and play an extra hole after which the error is discovered – the extra hole result counts because no claim was made before play commenced on the 19th tee (D2.5/6)*
- *players mistakenly misinterpret rules as a result of which A wins the hole. Mistake discovered before playing from the next tee and B should have won the hole. B cannot make a claim as they had agreed the result of the hole so there was no longer a dispute. The agreement of the wrong interpretation of the rules was not an offence as they had agreed in good faith (D2.5/8.5)*

Procedure

to be valid the player must notify his opponent that he is making
a claim, the facts on which he bases the claim and that he wants
a ruling. He must do so before he or his opponent plays from
the next teeing ground or if on the last hole before leaving the
putting green

Exceptions

1 late claims can be considered if based on facts previously
   unknown to the claimant who had also been given wrong
   information – see **Wrong information (w8)** (R34.1a)

2 after the result has been officially announced a claim cannot
   be considered unless the opponent knew he was giving
   wrong information (d) (R34.1a)

(d) late claims
   • *match won at 14th hole but before leaving*
   the 15th green the loser discovered the winner had breached
   the 14 club rule – a claim was made and because it was
   based on facts previously unknown the result was reversed –
   the match had to be resumed at the 15th (D2.5/5.5)
   • *even when player posted wrong score and it was pointed*
   out to him after result announced – wrong score stood
   because player did not record wrong score 'knowingly'
   (D2.5/11)
   • *'officially announced' usually means when the result is*
   posted on the official scoreboard. The official scoreboard
   may be a sheet of paper (D2.5/14)

Basic rules

1. on the putting green a ball may be lifted and cleaned at any time (R16.1b)

2. elsewhere on the course it may only be cleaned (a) when lifting is specifically permitted under an applicable Rule or local rule – see **Lifting the ball (l14)**

Exceptions

the ball may not be cleaned (R21) when it has been lifted:
(i) to determine if it is unfit for play see **Ball damaged (b7)** (R5.3)
(ii) for identification in accordance with the procedure under R12.2
 – it can be cleaned only to the extent necessary to permit identification; the player must first advise his opponent/fellow competitor and may not clean the ball if it is in a hazard (see **(i2)**)
(iii) because it is interfering with or assisting play (R22) – see **(b13)**
(iv) in a bunker
(v) to determine if it is embedded, in an aeration hole or in a hole made by a burrowing animal (D25.2/2)

a **cleaned – (when lifting was not permitted)**
 • *removing lime picked up from marking lines –*
 1 stroke penalty *(D21/1)*
• *removing grass or other loose impediments –*
 1 stroke penalty *(D21/2)*
• *ball accidentally cleaned – e.g. when caddie throws it to the player – it is a question of fact but any doubt is to be resolved against the player (D21/3)*
• *rubbing the ball on the green to clean it is acceptable provided it is not deemed testing the surface (D16.1d/5)*

Procedure

the ball should be marked, lifted, cleaned and then replaced on the spot from which it was lifted

– see **Marking the ball (m2), Lifting the ball (l14),** and **Placing/replacing the ball (p8)** for relevant procedures and penalties

Penalty

1 stroke – for breach of the rule (R21)

Exceptions

if the player incurs a penalty under the applicable Rule for breach of procedure in determining whether the ball is unfit for play, identifying the ball or because it is interfering or assisting with play he will not incur a further penalty under Rule 21 if he also cleans it

Acapulco Princess
GC, Mexico

C9 CLUB

What is it?

1 an implement conforming with the characteristics and
specifications (see Basic rules) in the Rules and designed
to be used for striking the ball. Clubs are generally classified
as woods, irons, wedges or putters

2 a club comprises a shaft and head fixed so that it is one unit.
It must not be adjustable except for weight (see **Putter (p17)**)
nor substantially different from the traditional and customary
form and make)

Basic rules 1

alterations to a club
(i) the playing characteristics of a club may not be purposely
altered (a) during a stipulated round (R4.2)
(ii) any part of a club which has been altered is deemed new and
must conform to the Rules (R4.1b)

a altering playing characteristics
• bandaid plaster stuck on to prevent
glare from sun does not alter playing
characteristics (D4.2/1)
• lie of clubs changed whilst play suspended –
disqualified if carried during the rest of the
round (D4.2/2)
• lead tape added before a round to adjust
weight – **no penalty** – but **disqualified** if
added during round (D4.2/0.5)

Basic rules ②

borrowing clubs

a player may only normally do so during a stipulated round ⓑ within the circumstances permitted under the rules relating to number (see **Basic rule 6**) and may only borrow clubs which do not form part of the 14 selected by another player for use during the round; a player may borrow a ball from another player (D5.1/5)

Basic rules ③

changing clubs

a player may only normally do so during a stipulated round within the circumstances permitted ⓑ under the rules relating to damage and number (see **Basic rules 5 and 6**)

ⓑ **permitted**
- may change between rounds in a 36 hole match as this is deemed 2 separate rounds (D4.4a/8)
- may change prior to a play off in a stroke play match as this is deemed a separate round (D4.4a/9)
- wet grip is not a valid reason to change clubs (D4.3/5) but loose grip is (R4.3/a)

Basic rules ④

conforming clubs

a player must play with clubs which conform ⒸC to the Rule 4 specifications. If there is any doubt whether a club manufactured or to be manufactured conforms a ruling from the R&A/USGA should be obtained (R4)

Penalty

for carrying (even though not used) a non conforming club – **disqualification** (D4.1/1)

Ⓒ conforms
• club which conforms when new is deemed to conform after normal wear (R4.1/2)

ⓓ damage
• must be substantial i.e. dented, loose, bent or broken – not merely scratched or an altered loft/lie (R4.3a)

ⓔ during normal course of play
• player putted with bent putter damaged in anger – **disqualified** (D4.3/4)
• NB putter damaged as above and replaced when player only had 13 clubs in his bag – **no penalty** – he was deemed merely adding a club (D4.3/8)
• damage occurred on practice ground during official suspension of play – club can be replaced (D4.4a6.5)
• normal course of play means when related to making a swing or stroke - not in searching, feeling or removing a club from bag (D4.3/1) or repairing a club damaged during normal play (D4.3/3)

What is it?

Basic rules

Basic rules ⑤

damaged club

if a club ceases to conform because of damage ⓓ during the
normal course of play ⓔ the player may: (R4.3)

(i) continue to use it for the remainder of the stipulated round **or**

(ii) repair it if this does not change the club's characteristics or
unduly delay play (R4.3c) **or**

(iii) if the damage renders it unfit for play he may replace it
provided he does not unduly delay play

If damage is sustained other than in the normal course of play the
club cannot be used or replaced during the remainder of the
round if broken during a stroke - see **Stroke (s26)**.

Penalty

for using a non conforming club – **disqualification**

Exceptions

– accidental damage caused to the club when it is used otherwise
than as a club -it may be replaced **without penalty** ⓕ

– for damage occurring during the course of a stroke and
affecting the validity of the stroke

– see **Stroke – exception (s26)**

– damage caused by outside agency e.g. greenkeeper's vehicle –
may repair, use or replace the club without penalty (D4.3/9.5)

ⓕ **otherwise than as a club**
• *putter accidentally damaged when
used as a walking stick during a round
cannot be replaced **without penalty** –
as it was not damaged during the normal
course of play (D4.3/7)*

Basic rules

Basic rules ⑥

number of clubs

the player:

(i) must start the round (g) with not more than 14 clubs (R4.4a)

(ii) must declare an excess (h) club out of play immediately on discovery

(iii) may without unduly delaying play make up the number if he started with fewer than 14 (i) (R4.3)

(iv) may replace any club with any other club if it becomes unfit for play during normal course of play (i) (R4.4a)

(v) may not replace a club from a 14 club bag for any reason other than that it is unfit for play (D4.3/10) even a lost club

(vi) may replace a club from a 13 (or fewer) club bag for any reason as this is deemed adding a club provided it does not unduly delay play

(vii) may share clubs with his partner provided the combined total of their clubs does not exceed 14 (R4.4b)

(viii) may borrow a club from another player unless that other player intended to use it as one of his 14 chosen clubs

(ix) may borrow a putter for a practice stroke because the stroke does not count for scoring purposes (D4.4a/13)

(g) **start**
• rule takes effect when the first stroke is played (D4.4a/1)

(i) **replace**
• addition or replacement may not be by borrowing clubs from another player's selected clubs (R4.4a) (D4.4a/12)
• may replace with a club previously declared out of play because it was 'excess' (D4.4c/2)

What is it?

Basic rules

h **excess**
• clubs carried for fellow competitor who has retired from the round are not excess provided they are not used *(D4.4a/3)*
• clubs carried for partner in foursomes are not excess provided each player's clubs are clearly identifiable *(D4.4a/4)*
• club put in another's bag by mistake after the commencement of a round is not excess – **penalty** only if used by the other player *(D4.4a/5)*
• but if put in before the round by mistake – **penalty** against the other player – *D4.4a/6*
• club found on the course added to 14 in the bag – **no penalty** *(D4.4a/8)*
• excess club taken from bag and declared out of play prior to commencement of round but carried on golf cart – **penalty** for starting with more than 14 clubs *(D4.4c/1)*

Penalty

match play – deduct **one hole** for each hole at which a breach occurred – **maximum penalty 2 holes**. The penalty is not applied against specific holes but to the state of the match after the conclusion of the hole at which the breach is discovered *(D4.4c/9)*

stroke play – **add 2 strokes** for each hole at which a breach occurred – **maximum penalty 4 strokes**

stableford – **deduct 2 points** for each hole at which a breach occurred – **maximum penalty 4 points**

failing to declare an excess club out of play – **disqualification** *(R4.4c)*

j **application of penalty**
• if breach discovered prior to a stroke being played on the tee – no breach at that hole *(D4.4a/11)*
• if breach occurs at more than 2 holes – penalty strokes are deemed added at the 1st and 2nd holes *(D4.4a/10)*

What is it?

131

What is it? – characteristics

face
– must be hard, rigid, have no concavity and roughness to be no greater than that of decorative sandblasting and neither material nor construction must impart significantly more spin than a standard steel face or have any other effect which would unduly influence the movement of the ball. (R4.1 and Appendix II)
– no markings are allowed on the impact area except grooves, punch marks and decorative markings within the parameters set out in Appendix II of the Rules
– markings restrictions do not apply to clubs with a non metallic impact area and loft of 24 degrees or less unless they unduly influence the movement of the ball (R4.1e)
– no foreign material may be applied to the club face for the purpose of influencing the movement of the ball (R4.3) e.g.chalk (D4.3/1) saliva (D4.3/2)

grip
– must be generally circular in cross section except for a continuous straight slightly raised rib along the full length of the grip. Diameter shall not exceed 1.75 inches (45mm). Grip may be tapered but must not have a bulge or waist. Axis of the grip must coincide with the axis of the shaft
– the grip may be changed if loose (D4.4a/2) but may not be changed during a round when wet/slippery (D4.4a/1) – **penalty for changing disqualification**

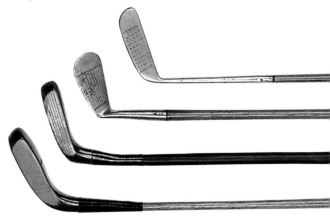

head
– generally plain in shape with all parts rigid, structural in nature and functional. Holes windows, fins plates and rods are not permitted (R4.1d). Woods must not be wider than 5 inches (127mm) heel to toe or 2.8 inches (71.12mm) sole to crown or greater than 28.06 cubic inches (460cc) face surface.

neck
– must not be more than 5 inches (127mm) in length from top of neck to sole of club measured along its axis. Shaft and neck must remain in line with heel (or point to right or left of it) when club is in the address position. Distance between axis of the shaft/neck and the back of the heel must not exceed 0.625 inches (16mm)

shaft
– at least 18 inches (457mm) long and generally straight from top of the grip to a point not more than 5 inches (127mm) above the sole. Bending and twisting properties must be consistent along its length (R4.1b). Maximum overall length of club must not exceed 48 inches (1219.2mm)

rule
– device on the shaft which emits a click if the swing is correctly timed – penalty – disqualification (D14.3/10)
  – see **Artificial devices (a12)**

C10 CLUB HOUSE

see *Obstruction – immoveable* (o3)

C11 CLUB LENGTH

What is it?

the means of measuring the distance from a defined point where under the Rules a player is permitted to drop or place the ball as required by the Rules

Basic rule

a player may use any club he has selected for the round for measuring a club length but must use the same club for all measuring in any given situation (D20/1)

Exception

when ascertaining the nearest point of relief from an immoveable obstruction the player must use the club he intends to use for his next stroke (D24.2b/3)

– see *Obstruction – immoveable* (o3)

The relief is within one club length and the ball may then roll a further two club lengths from where it strikes the course

Procedure

1 obviously it will be advantageous to use the longest club – usually the driver or possibly a long handled putter

2 the ball is permitted to roll up to a further 2 club lengths from where it strikes the course provided it does not come to rest nearer the hole (R20.2c)

3 the ball may roll up to a further 2 club lengths whether the original relief is 1 club length or 2 (R20.2c (vi))

4 – see **Dropping and redropping the ball (d16)** for additional procedures

5 **if there is no penalty involved**
the permitted relief is usually **one club length** – e.g. when taking relief from
– a hole, cast or runway of burrowing animal, bird or reptile
– the wrong putting green
– casual water
– ground under repair
– an immoveable obstruction

if there is a penalty involved
the permitted relief is usually **two club lengths** e.g. when taking relief from
– the point where ball was declared unplayable
– a lateral water hazard

a **any club**
• if a player borrows a club in order to measure he is not penalised if he drops the ball within an area which could have been measured with one of his own clubs but **loss of hole/ 2 stroke penalty** if he drops in an area which could not have been reached with one of his own clubs (D20/2)

135

COLOURBALL

a team game with teams of 3 or 4 in which one player plays a coloured ball. Team score comprises the score with the coloured ball plus the best of the other 2 or 3. Players alternate holes playing the coloured ball

 COMMITTEE

What is it?

the collective name for those in charge of a competition or, if no competition, those in charge of the course (DF)

Basic rules

1 it has no power to waive the rules of golf (R33.1)

2 it may appoint a referee to make decisions on its behalf on disputes and rules interpretations

3 its decisions are final (in the absence of a referee) (R34.3)

4 if it cannot reach a decision it should refer it to the Rules Of Golf Committee of the R&A/USGA and if the Committee fails to do so the players can do so through the club secretary (R34.3)

Procedure

its duties are to:
- define accurately the course, out of bounds, water hazards, lateral water hazards, ground under repair, obstructions (R33.2a)
- make new holes on competition days (R33.2b)
- make available a practice ground (R33.2c)
- make decisions as to whether the course is playable and organise suspensions and resumptions of play as necessary (R33.2d)
- organise starting times and group pairings (R33e)
- publish a table of holes where handicap strokes are to be taken (R33.4)
- issue score cards for competitions with date and players name
- in stroke play check the addition of scores and application of handicaps (a committee cannot delegate this to a player (D33.1/7))
- in stableford check the result of each hole, handicap application and total points (R33.5)
- arrange the resolution of halved matches by match play and ties by stroke play (R33.6)
- impose modify or waive the disqualification penalty if in exceptional circumstances it considers such action warranted – it may not alter any other penalty (R33.7)
- make and publish local rules consistent with those set out in the Rules of Golf (R33.8) including matters relating to:
  obstructions, roads and paths, preservation of the course, water hazards, boundaries and margins, dropping areas, temporary conditions, lifting a ball, practice between holes, preferred lies, winter rules, temporary obstructions

C14 COMPETITOR

a player in a stroke play competition (DF)

C15 CONCEDE

What is it?

match play term for giving a hole, stroke or match to an opponent

Basic rules

1. in match play a player can concede a stroke, the hole or the match – the last two may be at any time prior to completion of the hole (b) or the match (c)

2. the concession may not be withdrawn or declined by the opponent (R2.4)

3. once a concession is made generally subsequent events are irrelevant e.g. if the player then chooses to putt and misses (D2.4/7)

(b) completion of the hole

NB – ball found in hole after hole conceded – provided the claim was made before the next hole was commenced the concession was invalid as the hole was completed before the concession made (D2.4/11)

(c) completion of the match

• once a match is won, the winner cannot then concede it to his opponent e.g. because he cannot play in the next round (D2.4/19)

(a) concede

- *ball lifted after an ambiguous statement was wrongly interpreted as conceding a stroke – ball should be replaced and played (D2.4/3)*
- *concession given in ignorance of the rules is still valid (D2.4/12)*
- *concession given because of ignorance of the score is still valid (D2.4/14)*
- *concession may be implied – e.g. by player moving on to the next hole believing his ball had been lost (ball then found but play not allowed) (D2.4/13)*
- *concession of match made after completion of the match is invalid even though facts would have justified conceding if they had been known prior to completion of the match (D2.4/15)*
  NB but not if the irregularity claim is made within the time limits specified in the relevant rules (D2.4/16)
- *concession valid even though conceded because the date of play was inconvenient and the date was subsequently changed (D2.4/20)*

Hyatt la Manga GC, Spain

C16 CONFUSION

a game where one point is awarded to the first player of the group to be on the green, one for the player who is closest to the hole and one for the first player to hole out. The winner is the player with the highest number of points

C17 COURSE

the area within which play is permitted (DF)

C18 CRICKET

a game for three players where 6 points are scored on each hole – 4 for the lowest net score and 2 for the second lowest. For equal scores the points are shared. The winner is the player with the highest number of points

d1 DANGER

Basic rules

1 if a ball comes to rest in a dangerous ⓐ position e.g. by a bees nest or a snake the player is entitled to drop the ball **without penalty** at the nearest spot away from the danger (D1.4/10) but not nearer the hole

2 in a potentially dangerous situation the Committee may provide that play should be discontinued immediately
– see **Discontinuance/Lightning (d6)**

ⓐ **dangerous**
• refers to situations not normally encountered on a golf course – it does not apply to dangerous plants e.g. cactus or poison ivy etc (D1.4/11)

Procedure

see **Dropping the ball (d16)**

d2 DAYTONA

a game for 4 players divided into 2 sides. The scores of a side for each hole are combined to form a number of points; if one player has a score of par or better then the lower score of the team is placed first – if the scores on a par 3 are 3 and 4 then the team score is 34. But if the best score for the hole is over par then the higher must be placed first – if scores on a par 3 are 4 and 5 the team score is 54. The side with the lower number of points for the round wins

d3 DELAY

Basic rules

1 a player must at all times play and move between the green and next tee without undue delay **(a)** (R6.7) and the Committee may lay down pace of play guidelines in the rules of a competition

2 if a player is likely to delay the players behind – e.g. by searching for a lost ball – he should allow the group behind to play through (EQ) – on some courses rangers are employed to 'police' the pace of play and if they detect particularly slow play they may ask players to speed up the pace of play or to allow groups behind to play through

a undue delay
• *player on the green returns to the tee where he has left his putter* – **loss of hole/2 stroke penalty** *(D6.7/1)*
• *searching longer than 5 minutes for lost ball is undue delay* – **loss of hole/2 stroke penalty** *(D6.7/2)*
• *taking 45 minute break in clubhouse after 9 holes is deemed unauthorised discontinuance of play, not undue delay* – **disqualified** *(D6.8a/2)*
• *if motor cart breaks down and causes delay* – **no penalty** *(D6.8a/4)*
• *if the committee considers a player is guilty of undue delay it may intervene in a matchplay match (R.6.7)*
• *the committee may also intervene if it considers a player has exceeded the 5 minute lost ball rule as this is considered undue delay (DUS/34.3/101) (applicable in USA only)*

Penalty

loss of hole/2 strokes or if repeated breaches – **disqualification NB** the Committee may provide for the first offence – **1 stroke penalty**, for the second – **2 stroke penalty** and for the third – **disqualification** (R6.7). For breach of Basic rule **1** the penalty is applied to the next hole except in Stableford, bogey and par competitions where 2 points are deducted from the total score for the round (R6.7)

d4 DENVER

a game in Stableford format with amended points:–

8 points for 3 under par	0 points for par
5 points for 2 under par	-1 point for 1 over par
2 points for 1 under par	-3 points for 2 or more over par

d5 DEW

Basic rule

a player is not entitled to relief from dew on his line of play (R13.2) or putt (R16.1a) as it is not casual water

Penalty

for removing dew in breach of the rule – **loss of hole/2 strokes**

Exceptions

1 he may remove dew to the side of or from behind his ball

2 if dew is removed incidental to some permitted action such as removing loose impediments or repairing ball marks – **no penalty**

b **sudden illness /physical problem**
• *heat exhaustion, bee sting or struck by golf ball* – Committee should allow 10/15 minutes recuperation period (D6.8a/3)
• *because of breakdown of golf cart* – should report to Committee – **no penalty** recommended (D6.8a/5)

d6 DISCONTINUANCE OF PLAY

What is it?

a break in play which usually involves leaving the course. For shorter breaks which do not involve leaving the course see Delay **(d3)**

Basic rules

1 **by the Committee** – discontinuance may be ordered for any reason and in a potentially dangerous situation they may provide that play should be discontinued immediately (a)

2 **by a player** – he may discontinue the round **without penalty** if:

(i) he believes he is in danger from lightning (see **Lightning (l15)**) not just bad weather

(ii) he is seeking a decision from the Committee on a doubtful/disputed point

(iii) there is some other good reason such as sudden illness, fog or darkness (b)

(iv) taking a short (5 minute) refreshment break after 9 holes or if the committee allows a similar break in extremely hot or cold conditions (D6.8a/2.5/7)

(a) **immediately**
• Committee should arrange for a siren to be sounded (D6.8b/7) – if after that a player
• selects a club and plays within 30 seconds or taps in a short putt – **disqualified**
• but if having addressed the ball during the siren he plays his stroke quickly – **no penalty**
• discontinuance implies not playing further strokes. If a player takes a drop after discontinuance but does not play a stroke no penalty is incurred (D6.8b/8)

Penalty ➤

Exception ➤

Procedure ➤

145

d6 Discontinuance of play

Penalty

for unauthorised discontinuance or resumption – **disqualification**

Exception

in match play the players may discontinue by agreement (C) unless this causes delay to the entire competition (R6.8a)

(C) agreement
- players agreed to discontinue because of heavy rain – subsequently A proposes to resume but B objects because it is still raining – B **disqualified** because there was no longer an agreement to discontinue (D6.8a/5)
- players agreed to discontinue because of heavy rain – subsequently A proposes to resume but B objects because he considers the course unplayable – they should refer to the Committee – if Committee uphold B's claim the match should be resumed when the course is playable; if not B should be disqualified (D6.8a/6)

Procedure

1 if discontinued by the player he should report to the Committee as soon as practicable and if the reason is acceptable there is **no penalty** (R6.8a)

2 if the players are in the process of playing a hole they **(d)** may discontinue immediately or when the hole is completed but without undue delay

(d) they
- If in match play one wishes to discontinue immediately and the other finish the hole, they should both discontinue, but if one insists on continuing he should not be disqualified, but should incur the loss of hole penalty (D6.8b/3.5)

What is it

Basic rules

146

3 (i) if play is discontinued by the committee – before completing the hole the ball may be marked, lifted and cleaned; on resumption it should be replaced in its original spot (R6.8c) – if not marked – **1 stroke penalty** (D6.8c/2) (see *Dropping and redropping the ball* **(d16)** for procedures)

(ii) if discontinued by the player he may not lift his ball without good reason i.e. if it is likely that the ball may be moved or taken by an outside agency (D6.8c/1)

4 (i) play may only be resumed when the Committee so orders (R6.8b)

(i) the player is entitled to resume with the lie which he had when play was discontinued (f)

(iii) if the player lifted the bill it must be replaced on the same spot.

(iv) if he did not lift it, he may mark it, lift it and clean it before resuming (R6.8d) If he moves the ball before marking it he is penalised – see **b18(v)** *Ball moved by player* (D18.2a/25)

e **resume**
• if a player cannot play when play is resumed the following day after a discontinuance – **disqualified** (D6.8b/4)
• due to reasonable mistake a player restarts 2 minutes before the official resumption – Committee should allow 5 minutes early or late without disqualifying but may impose or modify the penalty if appropriate (D6.8b/6)
• players who restarted before authorised by the Committee – **disqualified** (D6.8b/1)

f **same lie**
• ball moved by wind/rain during discontinuance/suspension – player is entitled to replace **without penalty** (D18.1/11)
• lie worsened by natural causes - ball may not be moved elsewhere (D6.8d/1)

d7 DISQUALIFICATION

What is it?

the most severe of the penalties imposed by the Rules. A player may be disqualified from the event ⓐ or in match play from the event or from the hole. See **Penalties (p5)** for a list of offences which warrant disqualification

> **ⓐ disqualified**
> • if a player is disqualified from an event he forfeits right to prizes won in the event prior to disqualification e.g. long drive prize (D33.7)
> • but a player disqualified from a handicap event because he played off the wrong handicap was entitled to win the lowest gross score prize as his breach of the rules was not relevant to a gross score event (D33.1/13)

Procedure

a player may only be disqualified after a competition has closed:
(i) if he has returned a score lower than that taken, or
(ii) if he knowingly declared a wrong handicap, or
(iii) if he agreed to waive a rule

d8 DISTANCE MARKERS

posts or other objects placed on the course to indicate the distance to the green. They are one of the few artificial devices permitted under the Rules to aid assessment of distance (D33.5)

d9 DISTRACTION

caused by anything from a ball dropped on the teeing area to an earthquake is not grounds for for any relief such as replaying the shot (D1.4/1)

Moon Valley GC, Arizona

d10 DIVOT

a piece of turf dislodged or removed during the making of a stroke

1. a detached divot is a loose impediment (see **Loose impediment (l9)**) and can be replaced **without penalty** but may not be pressed down if this would improve the player's lie/line of putt or area of intended swing ⓐ (D13.2/6)

2. a divot which is not completely detached is not a loose impediment and therefore cannot be removed or replaced even if it interferes with a player's swing or line of putt (D13.2/5) – if removed – **penalty 2 strokes/loss of hole**

ⓐ **improving his lie**
   • *if a player replaces a divot and subsequently finds he must drop a ball on the spot e.g. because his ball went out of bounds there is **no penalty** for improving his lie by having replaced the divot (D13.2/4.5)*

Procedure

1 a divot need not be replaced in the hole from which it came (D13.2/7)

2 a divot from an opponent's stroke came to rest adjacent to a player's ball in a bunker – he may remove it **without penalty** as he is entitled to his original lie (D13.4/18)

3 any divots made by a player after a stroke through the green should be replaced and pressed down (EQ)

4 a ball coming to rest in a divot hole must be played as it lies

d11 DOG

What is it?

see **Outside agency (o6)** for rules purposes

Procedure

1. most golf clubs do not allow pet dogs to be taken on the golf course

2. if a dog moves a golf ball:
   see **Ball deflected (b8)** – if the ball was moving at the time
   see **Ball moved (b18)** – if it was stationary at the time

d12 DORMIE

match play term when a side is as many holes up as there are holes to play (R2.1) i.e. the opponent/s cannot win

d13 DOUBLE BOGEY

a score of 2 strokes over par for a hole

d14 DOUBLE EAGLE

What is it?

a score of 3 under par for a hole. Scores 5 points in Stableford competition.

d15 DRESS

What is it?

what to wear on the course is not a subject of the Rules of Golf but is often determined by the individual golf clubs. Generally speaking dress should be casually smart and appropriate to the game of golf i.e. golf shoes, trousers (or skirts for the ladies), golf shirt, sweater and suitable outerwear/rainwear. Some clubs prohibit the wearing of shorts by men. Denim jeans, tee shirts and training shoes are generally not acceptable. Many clubs require jacket and tie (or the equivalent for ladies) in the clubhouse – particularly in an evening.

d16 DROPPING AND REDROPPING THE BALL

Basic rules ❶

when required by a Rule to be dropped the ball must not be dropped nearer the hole and must land on the applicable part of the course ⓐ – usually within 1 or 2 club lengths of, or 'as near as possible to' a point defined by the relevant Rule (R20.2b)

> ### ⓐ applicable part of the course
> • ball dropped and lands in a bush so it does not touch the ground – it must be played as it lies as the bush is part of the course (D20.2b/1)
> • ball dropped hits a bush and lands outside the dropping area – the bush is part of the course so play the ball as it lies unless it qualifies for a redrop (**NB** in calculating a 2 clubs length roll the player must measure from the point beneath where it hit the bush (D20.2c/1.3)
> • ball missed completely off the tee – second shot hit out of bounds – player may drop anywhere in the teeing ground (not as near as possible to where the previous stroke was played) (D20.5/1)
> • if the ball was in a bunker or other hazard it must be dropped in the same hazard or if not possible, in a similar hazard
> • if the applicable part of the course is in an area from which play is prohibited (e.g. ground under repair) the player may still drop the ball there but must take further relief as appropriate (D20.7/3)

Penalty

for breach of Basic rules ❶ or ❷ **loss – of hole/2 strokes**
for not redropping when required – **loss of hole/2 strokes**

Basic rules ②

a player must not improve or allow to be improved ⓑ the
area in which he is to drop or place his ball by (R13.2)
(i) moving bending or breaking anything growing or fixed including
immovable obstructions and objects defining out of bounds or
(ii) removing or pressing down sand loose soil replaced divots other
cut turf placed in position or other irregularities of surface or (iii)
removing dew, frost or water

Exceptions

improvement which may occur:

① in fairly taking his stance

② in making his stroke or the backward movement of his club
for a stroke

③ on the teeing ground in creating or eliminating irregularities
of surface

④ on the putting green in removing sand or loose soil or
repairing damage as permitted by R16 – see **(p18)**

⑤ in grounding the club which may only be done lightly and not
so as to press it against the ground (R13.2)

ⓑ **improve**
• caddie holds back a branch at the
spot where a player is to drop the ball
– deemed exerting influence on the
position of the ball under R1.2 –
penalty – loss of hole/2 stroke
(D20.2a/5) – see **(i9)**
• a player cannot remove sand or loose
soil from the dropping area (D13.2/11)

Basic rules

Exceptions

Procedure

Penalty

155

Basic rules

3 if a ball is dropped in the wrong place or placed when it should have been dropped provided it has not been played it can be lifted and redropped correctly **without penalty** (R20.6) **NB** if it has been played – **loss of hole/2 stroke penalty** (D3.3/3)

4 a ball **must** be redropped **without penalty** if it rolls (C):
(i) into a hazard
(ii) out of a hazard
(iii) on to a putting green
(iv) out of bounds (d)
(v) to a position where there is interference from the condition from which relief was taken under R24 (immovable obstruction) or R25 (**Animals** (see **(a10)**), **Casual water** (see **(c4)**), **Ground under repair** (see **(g9)**) or back into its own pitch mark) (e)
(vi) more than two club lengths (f) from where it first landed
(vii) nearer the hole than (x) its original position (y) the nearest point of relief (if Appropriate).

(d) **out of bounds**
• if having dropped the ball in bounds it comes to rest then rolls out of bounds before the stroke is played it cannot be redropped without penalty – the out of bounds procedure **(see O5)** must be followed (D20.2c/3.5)

(f) **two club lengths**
• if a rule allows a drop within two club's length of the problem, the ball may then roll up to 2 club lengths further and end up almost 4 club lengths from the original problem (D20.2c/1) – but not nearer the hole
• ball moved in measuring to determine if it had rolled more than 2 clubs length – **no penalty** – replace if within the distance – redrop it if outside the distance (D20.2c/6)

Basic rules

Penalty

C rolls

• if a caddie deliberately stops a dropped ball before it comes to rest, but after reaching one of the positions in Basic rule 4, because it would clearly require redrop – **no penalty** (D20.2c/4) but if it is stopped before it reaches one of the positions in Basic rule 4, even though it was obvious that it would reach such position – **penalty – loss of hole/2 strokes**

• no redrop is allowed if the ball is dropped directly into a hazard as opposed to rolling into it (D28.4/5)

e interference from the condition

• in determining both the point of relief from an immoveable obstruction and whether interference continues to exist the player should measure with the club he intends to use for the next stroke. If there is still interference he must redrop even though he could avoid the interference by using a different club (D20.2c/0.7). Having redropped he may use a different club to play his next stroke (D24.2b/4)

• ball dropped away from ground under repair landed where the

player had to stand in GUR to play it – redrop allowed (D20.2c/0.5)

• ball which rolls back into its own pitch mark should be redropped (R25.2c(v))

• interference refers not only to the position of the ball but also with the area of swing and player's stance (c.f. dropping as opposed to redropping)

When dropping within one or two club lengths, it is recommended that the extent of the club lengths be marked before dropping

Basic rules

Procedure

Penalty

Basic rules

5 if on redropping it rolls again as above then it should be placed **(g)** as near as possible to where it first landed when it was dropped (R20.2c) but if it comes to rest before rolling again it must be played as it lies

6 if a ball is dropped when not permitted by the rules e.g. away from an object in the mistaken belief that it is an immoveable obstruction – the player is penalised under the **Ball moved** (see **(b18)**) rules of Rule 18 – **1 stroke penalty** and if he does not replace it – a **further 1 stroke penalty/loss of hole** (D18.2a/3)

g   placed

• *if ball is redropped when it should be placed and the error is not corrected before the stroke is played –* **loss of hole/2 stroke penalty**

• *must redrop before being allowed to place even if it is obvious that the ball will roll again and qualify for placement* (D20.2c/3)

• *if in a bunker it cannot be dropped or placed because it always ends up nearer the hole it should be dropped* **under 1 stroke penalty** *behind the bunker on the extension of the line between the original spot and the hole* (D30.3d/2)

h   any other manner

• *putting spin on a ball when dropping it –* **1 stroke penalty** *for improper dropping* (D20.2a/2)

Basic rules

Penalty

Exception

Procedure

1. the player may remove loose impediments from the area in which he is to drop the ball (D23.1/6) but sand and loose soil are only loose impediments if on the putting green.

2. it is recommended that when a ball is to be dropped 'as near as possible' to a specific spot the player places a ball marker at that spot so that any disputes – such as the distance the ball has rolled – can be resolved easily

3. when a ball is required to be dropped within one or two club lengths, it is recommended that the extent or the one or two club lengths be marked with tees so that it can easily be determined whether the ball has rolled more or less than the further 2 club lengths permitted by the rules – see **Club length (c11)**

4. the ball must only be dropped by the player himself when standing erect by holding the ball at shoulder height and arm's length to the side or in front of the player – if it is done by any other person or in any other manner (h) and the error is not corrected – **1 stroke penalty** (R20.2a) (i)

(i) **application of the penalty**
• player dropped in the wrong manner and in the wrong place – errors not corrected – **1 stroke penalty** for improper drop plus **2 strokes** for breach of wrong place rule R25.1b (D20.2a/3)
• player dropped in the wrong manner and then the ball moved when addressed – player then redropped – **1 stroke penalty** as the ball was in play when first dropped and redropping did not cancel the penalty under R18.2b (D20.2a/4)

Procedure

Penalty

Procedure

5 if the exact spot for dropping/placing cannot be established e.g. because the marker has been moved, the ball must be dropped (or on the green placed) as near as possible to the original spot but not in a hazard or on a putting green (unless the ball was in a hazard/on a green in the first place)

6 the ball is permitted to roll up to two club lengths from the point where it landed on the course (j) – even if the relief allows a drop only within 1 club length

7 where the Committee has marked out a 'dropping zone' under a local rule the lines are within the zone and provided the ball first lands within the zone it may come to rest outside it (D33.8/34)

8 if on dropping the ball touches the player, his partner, either of their caddies or equipment before or after it touches the course it must be redropped (any number of times) **without penalty** (R20.2a)

9 if on dropping or redropping the ball is not easily recoverable another ball may be substituted (R20.2c)

Basic rules

Penalty

Exception

Procedure

Penalty

for breach of Procedure **1 stroke**

j **two club lengths**
- *if a rule allows a drop within two club's length of the problem, the ball may then roll up to 2 club lengths further and end up almost 4 club lengths from the original problem* (D20.2c/1) – *but not nearer the hole*
- *ball moved in measuring to determine if it had rolled more than 2 clubs length* – **no penalty** – *replace if within the distance* – *redrop it if outside the distance* (D20.2c/6)

McCormick Ranch GC, Arizona

What is it?

an area marked by the Committee where a player can take relief from an immoveable obstruction, ground under repair, a water hazard or if his ball is unplayable

Procedure

1. the player can stand anywhere but the ball must land first in the dropping zone

2. the ball may roll or bounce out of the zone must not come to rest more than 2 club lengths from where it first landed

3. the ball may roll nearer the hole than where it was when in its original position

4. if it rolls more than 2 club lengths, into a hazard, on to a green or out of bounds it should be redropped **without penalty**

5. where the Committee has marked out a 'dropping zone' under a local rule the lines are within the zone and provided the ball first lands within the zone it may come to rest outside it (D33.8/34)

e1 EAGLE

a score of two under par for a hole. Scores 4 points in Stableford competition

e2 ECLECTIC

an individual stroke play game comprising a defined number of rounds. At the end of the series each of the competitors records his best score of the series at each hole

e3 ELECTRICAL STORM

see *Lightning* (l15)

e4 ENVIRONMENTALLY SENSITIVE AREAS

1. should be designated and marked by the Committee as ground under repair, water hazards or lateral water hazards as appropriate

2. strokes played from them are penalised as per the relevant rules (D33.8/42-44)

   – see *Ground under repair* (g9), *Water hazard* (w2) and *Lateral water hazard* (l1) for the relevant rules and procedures

e5 EQUIPMENT

anything used (a) worn or carried by or for a player except his
ball in play (b) and any small object (c) when used to mark the
ball or the area in which a ball is to be dropped (DF)

for rules re unusual equipment see **Artificial devices (a12)**

for rules re ball hitting equipment see **Ball deflected (b8)** and

for equipment hitting a stationary ball see **Ball moved (b18)**

(a) anything used
- *shared golf cart and anyone or anything in it (D19/2) is deemed to be equipment of the player whose ball is involved in the problem situation except when it is being moved when it and everything in it are deemed to be the equipment of the driver (D18/8)*
- *balls other than a player's own ball in play are deemed to be equipment (DF)*

(b) ball in play
- *a ball which has been lifted is equipment until it is replaced; a provisional ball, second ball and a ball being used for practice is not equipment (D18/7)*

(c) small object
- *glove used to mark an area of drop is equipment not a small object (D18/9)*

e6 EQUITY

the means according to what is fair and reasonable (a) in the
circumstances of deciding any point in dispute which is not
covered by the Rules (R1.4)

(a) fair and reasonable
- *a ball struck in anger from the group behind towards the group ahead – **2 shot penalty/loss of hole** (D1.4/4)*
- *if a ball cannot be identified because of mud – lift **without penalty** and clean it to the extent necessary to identify it (D1.4/6)*
- *ball comes to rest in a dangerous position or in a bird's nest – free drop not nearer the hole (D1.4/9 and 10)*
- *ball stuck to wet sand on club – free drop (D1.4/2)*

e7 ETIQUETTE

What is it?

the standards of behaviour and consideration for other players that are expected of golfers on the golf course. If a player is guilty of persistent breaches the Committee may ban him from the course for a period of time or for a serious breach of etiquette he may be disqualified (R33.7)

Procedure

1. **spirit of the game;** players should always conduct themselves in a disciplined, courteous and sportsmanlike manner

2. **safety;** players should ensure that in practising or playing a stroke nobody is likely to be injured by the club, the ball or any debris which may be moved as a result of the stroke. If by chance a ball is hit in the direction of another person the warning 'Fore' should be shouted

3. **courtesy;** when another player is about to play a stroke others should not position themselves or behave in any way which might distract the player or disturb his concentration – including using mobile phones or other electronic devices

4. **care of the course;** players should rake bunkers after use and as far as possible play in such a manner that does not cause damage to the course, its flora and fauna; they should repair divots or other damage to the course made by them or their equipment within the limits permitted by the rules – see *Divot (d10)*, *Spike marks (s13)*, *Putting green (p18)*

5. **pace of play;** players should always play at a pace which does not delay or inconvenience others on the course – see *Delay (d3)* If the lost ball procedures are delaying the group behind then the player should wave them through

e8 EXCHANGING BALLS

for rules when a player inadvertently exchanges his ball with someone else's see **Ball changed (b4)** and **Ball exchanged (b10)**; for rules re exchanging the ball for another e.g. because it is damaged see **Substituting a ball (s31)**

The Old Course, St. Andrews, Scotland

FAIRWAY

the closely mown area of the course between the teeing area and the putting green. It is not per se the subject of any of the rules of golf

 # FELLOW COMPETITOR

stroke play term for any person with whom a competitor plays, but not a partner except in fourball/foursome matches (DF)

 # FENCE

see *Obstruction – immovable* (o3) and *Out of bounds* (o5)

 # FLAG COMPETITION

a stroke play game in which each player has a flag and when the player has played the number of strokes equal to the the par of the course plus his handicap he places a flag in the course at that point. The winner is the person who goes farthest round the course with his allotted strokes – in rare cases this may mean playing the first few holes a second time

Left: Aloha GC, Spain

f5 FLAGSTICK

What is it?

a moveable straight pole, circular in cross section (a), with or without material attached (b), centred in the hole to show its position (DF) – see **Attending the flagstick (a14)** and **Ball resting against flagstick (b20)**

(a) **circular**
- flagstick may be tapered or of varying diameter (D17/3)
- in the USA the USGA recommends that it is at least 7 feet high (D/US17/100)

(b) **material**
- an attachment to a flagstick to indicate the position of the hole on the green must be circular in cross section (D17/1)
- the use of coloured flags on flagstick to indicate position of the hole is acceptable (D17/2)

Procedure

1. if the flagstick is leaning a player may centre it but may not adjust it so that his ball would fall into the hole more easily if it hit it (D17/4)

2. it should be replaced in the hole before leaving the putting green (EQ)

3. ball lodged in the flag – should be placed on the lip of the hole – **no penalty** (D17/6) – see **Moveable obstructions (o3)**

4. ball hits the flagstick:
   (i) blown over by wind – **no penalty** (D17.3/3)
   (ii) removed by the group ahead who are still on the green – **no penalty** (D17.3/3)
   (iii) placed on the green by an opponent/fellow competitor – the player is penalised **loss of hole/2 stroke penalty** (D17.3/3)

(iv) when attended – see *Attending the flagstick* **(a14)**

(v) when unattended **2 stroke penalty** if the ball was on the putting green when the stroke was played – if off the green **no penalty** (R17.3c)

5 flagstick dropped by a player moves the ball – **1 stroke penalty** unless done whilst measuring distances to determine the order of play (D18.2a/24)

6 flagstick moved on the green to prevent a ball hitting it – person moving it **loses hole/2 stroke penalty** (D1.2/3) but no penalty if the person moving it had been attending it (D17.1/6) or if he had not been attending it but was still holding it (D17.1/8)

7 flagstick stuck in the green away from the hole – no relief (D1.4/3)

f6 FOG

see *Discontinuance of play (d6)*

f7 FORE

the conventional shouted warning to other players that they are in danger of being hit by a golf ball. If players hear the shout they should take evasive action immediately!

f8 FORECADDIE

a person employed by the Committee to indicate to players the position of balls during play. Deemed to be an outside agency

What is it?

a match play or stroke play game when two ('a side') score (a) their **Better ball** (see **(b25)**) against the better ball of the other two (DF)

Variations

1. **Fourball Aggregate** – when the combined scores of the side count as opposed to the better ball counting

2. **High and Low** – points game with the player with the lowest net score of the four on each hole scoring a point for his side and the player with the highest net score losing a point for his side. Equal high or low scores – no points

(a) score
- the gross score of whichever partner's score is to count should be recorded against his name for each hole (R31.4)
- marker put gross 4 for partner A but no gross score, only a net 3 for partner B – 4 was counted and not 3 – it was the players duty to check the scorecard and it was the Committee's duty to extract the better ball scores from the recorded gross scores (D31.4/1)
- marker recorded a 6 for a player who had in fact picked up – partner scored lower gross of 5 – **no penalty** as disqualification only applies if a wrong score is recorded as the sides score (D31.7a/1)
- marker recorded 4 against a player who had picked up instead of against his partner who had in fact scored 4 – side was **disqualified** even though 4 was the correct team score for the side (D31.7a/2)

Procedure →

Penalties →

Left: Kananaskis GC, Canada

Procedure

1 a side may be represented at any time by one or more of the partners – an absent partner may join the match between holes but not during the play of a hole ⓐ (R30.3a/R31.2)

2 a side can play in any order it chooses ⓑ (R30.3c/R31.5) – provided this does not unduly delay play

3 only one partner need sign the team card (R31.4)

4 the marker need record only one score - the qualifying gross score - at each hole but he must indicate which partner made that score. He need not record both scores at each hole (R31.4)

ⓐ **during play**
• if a partner joins in during the play of a hole he is **disqualified** for that hole – if his play assists his partner he is also **disqualified** (D30.3a/1) but he can give his partner advice (D30.3a/2)

ⓑ **order of play**
• on the putting green a side may play in any order even if it involves the ball nearest the hole being played first and a player standing on the line of another players putt (D30.3c/1)
• if both members of a side play in the wrong order their opponents can only require the second person to replay his ball (R10.1c) (D30.1/1)

Penalties

1 normal penalties apply according to the rules which have been broken and apply only against the partner who incurred the penalty except as specified in ❸ – ❻ opposite

What is it?

174

2 in fourball match play if the penalty is loss of hole it is interpreted as disqualifying the offender from the hole – but not his partner (R30.3f) Ⓒ

3 in stroke play or match play **the side is disqualified** from the competition if <u>one</u> partner breaches the rules relating to (R30. 3e): –

agreements to waive rules
applying foreign material to clubs
changing the characteristics of a ball
changing the characteristics of clubs
conforming clubs
conforming ball
having more than one caddie
playing off a higher handicap
repeated undue delay
use of artificial devices/unusual equipment

4 in stroke play or match play **the side is disqualified** from the competition if <u>both</u> partners breach rules relating to (R30.3d/31.7b): –
time of starting
discontinuance of play

5 in stroke play only **the side is also disqualified from the competition** if <u>one</u> partner breaches rules relating to (R31.7a): –
practice before/between rounds
refusal to comply with rules
score card irregularities

6 for breach of the 14 club rules by either partner, the side is penalised as per rules

Penalty Ⓒ

C application of penalties

- *player and partner both in a bunker – player lifted loose impediment which improved his partner's lie –* **both disqualified** (D30.3f/1)

- *player failing to inform his opponents of a penalty led them to pick up in the belief they had lost the hole – deemed to have adversely affected their play, so partner* **disqualified** *as well* (D30.3f/3)

- *player deliberately putted away from the hole to be on the same line as his partner so he could assist his partner by showing him the line of putt – deemed contrary to the spirit of the game -* **disqualified** *in match play or in stroke play* **2 stroke penalty** *for player and partner* (D30.3f/6)

- *player requested his opponent to lift a ball on the green as it might assist opponent's partner – opponent refused – opponent* **disqualified** *under R22 and if the infringement did assist his partner – he was* **also disqualified** *under R30.3f* (D30.3f/11)

- *player putted his partner's ball –* **disqualified** *– opponents claimed the partner was also disqualified as the player's putt had assisted play in giving him the line – not upheld* (D30.3d/1)

- *as above but opponents claimed failure to inform them of the breach entitled them to the hole – not upheld* (D30.3d/3.5)

- *player putted partner's ball but error not discovered until on the next tee – late claim by opponents was valid as the player had given wrong information as to his score – player* **disqualified** *from the hole* (D30.3d/2)

- *player and opponent played each other's balls on the putting green – the two partners picked up – error discovered on the next tee – player and opponent were* **disqualified** *and the partner who picked up first* **lost the hole** (D30.3d/3)

- *if a wrong ball is played except in a hazard –* **2 stroke penalty** *and must play the correct ball – but* **no penalty** *against the partner* (R31.6) (stroke play)

- *if a player plays a wrong ball except in a hazard he is* **disqualified for the hole** *but his partner is not penalised (match play) – if the wrong ball belongs to his partner/opponent he must place the ball on the spot from which the wrong ball was played* (R30.3d)

What is it?

a match play or stroke play game when two play against two others and each side (a) plays one ball (DF)

1 **Threesome** – when two play against one other and each side plays one ball

2 **American Foursome** – each player plays his own ball from the tee and then they hit each other's second shot before choosing the better placed ball to complete the hole

3 **Canadian Foursome** – each player plays his own ball from the tee and also for the second shot before choosing the better placed ball to complete the hole

4 **Greensome** – as above but the choice is made after the drive

5 **Gruesome** – as above but they choose the worse drive

(a) **side**
• *the composition of teams may not be changed after the first side has played from the tee* (D29/1)

Procedure

Penalty

Basic rule

as this is a team game for rules purposes the offences of the
partner are those of the player and vice versa (b)

> (b) **example**
> • the player played a bunker shot and having failed
> to get out then hit the sand in disgust – as his partner
> still had to play from the bunker this was deemed
> touching the ground in the hazard – see **Bunker (b33)**
> and the side suffered the **loss of hole penalty** (D29/5)

Procedure

1. the partners play strokes alternately (c) from each teeing
ground and during the play of each hole (R29.1) so if an even
number of strokes are taken for the hole the same person
will hole out at one hole and then tee off at the next hole

2. either partner may sign the scorecard (D29/6)

Penalties

for playing in the wrong order

match play – **loss of hole** (R29.2)

stroke play – the stroke is cancelled, a **2 stroke penalty** is
incurred and the side must play in the correct order from the
spot where the incorrect stroke was played – if this is not
corrected before playing from the next teeing ground or if on
the last hole before leaving green – the side is **disqualified**

What is it?

C **alternately**

   • *penalty strokes are not deemed strokes for the purpose of the order of play*

• *player accidentally moves his ball after address –* **1 stroke penalty** *but he must replace and replay it, not his partner* (D29.1/5)

• *mixed team – man plays from the tee and goes out of bounds – lady must play the next stroke from the men's tee* (D29/2)

• *where rules require a drop to be taken – the player to play the stroke must drop the ball* (D29/4)

• *stroke played outside the teeing ground is not deemed a stroke for purposes of the order of play – the original player has to replay it, not his partner* (D29.1/1)

• *if a partner does play it the* **penalty is 2 strokes** *for playing outside the teeing ground* **plus 2 strokes** *for playing in the wrong order* (D29.1/2) *– the stroke must then be replayed from within the teeing ground – if not –* **disqualified**

• *provisional ball must be played by the partner* (D29.1/3)

• *if not and the original ball is lost the provisional becomes the ball in play –* **loss of hole/2 stroke penalty** (D29.1/4)

• *wrong partners on both sides in match play drive off at the same hole – the side which played first loses the hole* (D29.2/1)

• *poor player deliberately missed the ball so his partner could play a difficult shot over water – not deemed a stroke as he had no intention of moving the ball –* **loss of hole/2 stroke penalty** *if his partner subsequently played the stroke because the partners had then changed the order of play* (D29.1/7). *In stroke play, the poor player must play again – if not,* **both disqualified**

• *partners drive in the wrong order for 3 holes in match play – error not noticed by their opponents until 3rd hole – opponents cannot claim the first 2 holes because they should have realised the wrong order and had not made a valid claim – they can claim the 3rd hole* (D29.2/2)

FREE DROP

when dropping the ball is permitted **without penalty** in
accordance with the Rules e.g. when a ball is embedded
in its own pitch mark in the fairway

 FRINGE

the area surrounding the putting green which is sometimes cut
to a height lower than the fairway but not as closely as the green
itself. It is not recognised by the rules and for rules purposes must
be treated as *Through the green* (see **(t10)**) and not as part of
the green unless otherwise provided in a local rule (D33.8/33)

 FROST

see *Dew* **(d5)**

FULL HOUSE

game in which a player is set a points target calculated by
deducting his handicap from 36. The winner is the player who
exceeds his target by most points. Scoring is 8 points for an
eagle, 4 for a birdie, two for par and 1 for bogey

g

g1 GAMBLING

there are no rules relating to gambling – but the following are
relevant policy statements:

1. gambling is acceptable if limited to the players themselves
   or their teams and the money is put up by the players
   themselves provided always that the primary purpose of
   the game is enjoyment

2. breaches are treated as infringements of the amateur
   status rules

3. the governing authorities disapprove of calcuttas, auction
   sweepstakes and the like organised for general participation

4. if a club consistently permits competitions where excessive
   gambling is involved it may be subject to sanctions by the
   relevant national golf union

g2 GOLF

the game consists of playing a ball from the teeing ground into
the hole by a stroke or successive strokes in accordance with
the Rules (R1.1)

g3 GOLF BAG

is deemed to be *Equipment* (see **(e5)**). For rules and procedures
when a ball hits a golf bag – see *Ball deflected* **(b8)**
or when a golf bag hits a ball – see *Ball moved* **(b18)**

g4 GOLF SHOES

see *Dress* **(d15)** and *Spikes* **(s14)**

g5 GRASS CUTTINGS

Basic rules

1. they are **Ground under repair** (see **(g9)**) even though not marked if they are piled for removal, but not if scattered or abandoned and not intended to be removed unless specifically marked as GUR

2. they may always be treated as **Loose impediments** (see **(l19)**) (D25/11)

g6 GREEN

see **Putting green (p18)**

g7 GREENSOME

see **Foursome (f10)**

g8 GROSS SCORE

the actual number of strokes taken by a player or side for a hole or round before deducting any handicap allowance

g9 GROUND UNDER REPAIR (GUR)

see **Abnormal Ground Conditions (a1)**

g10 GROUNDING THE CLUB

see **Addressing the ball (a2)**

h₁ HALF

What is it?

the term to denote that each player or side has scored the same number of strokes for a hole (R2.2)

Procedure

in match play if one player holes out leaving his opponent 1 stroke to halve the hole and the player then incurs a penalty e.g. for giving advice to his opponent – the hole is deemed halved even if the opponent misses the putt (D2.2/1)

h₂ HANDICAP

What is it?

the means of enabling players of unequal abilities to compete against each other on equal standing usually and initially by measuring their respective abilities against the **Standard scratch score** (see **(s20)**) for their respective home courses. It does not take account of the differences in difficulty between their respective home courses and is subsequently adjusted by the club's handicap committee by a complex formula based on the results posted in qualifying competitions or rounds

Left: Hilton Head South Carolina

What is it?

Basic rule

Procedure

Penalty

Exceptions

1. the calculation of men's and ladies' handicaps is by reference to different systems in different countries

2. players are given an exact handicap calculated to one decimal place and a playing handicap rounded to the nearest whole number – 0.5 is rounded upwards

3. the maximum handicap for men is 28 and for ladies 45

Basic rules

1. in *match play* it is a player's responsibility to know the holes at which strokes are given or received for himself and his opponent – but the onus is on the opponent to question any strokes believed to have been wrongly taken (a) (R6.2a)

2. in *stroke play*:
   (i) a competitor must ensure his handicap is correctly recorded on the score card before it is returned to the Committee (R6.2b)
   (ii) BUT it is the Committee's responsibility to ensure scores are correctly added and the handicap correctly applied (R33.5)

   – see also *Scorecard* **(s3)** for relevant rules and decisions

What is it?

a **strokes wrongly taken**
• *handicap properly declared at the beginning but a stroke was taken at the wrong hole – an opponent cannot make a claim (match play) unless made before play at the hole after the one where the error was made – it was the opponent's duty to see that strokes were taken at the correct holes* (D2.5/13)
NB *by mistake a stroke was not taken and the hole conceded; error noticed before play commenced at next hole hole – no adjustment allowed* (D6.2a/4) *as the concession could not be withdrawn –* see **Concede (c15)**
• *by mistake a stroke was taken at the wrong hole and the error not noticed until after the round was completed – result stands as played* (D6.2a/2)
• *by mistake a stroke was taken at the wrong hole and the error noticed before the hole was completed – score should be adjusted with* **no penalty** (D6.2a/3)
• *by mistake wrong handicap allowance was used in match play – full instead of 3/4 – result stands as played* (D6.2a/6).
• *in foursomes one side correctly recorded their combined handicaps on the card –* **disqualified** *for not recording their individual handicaps* (D6.2b/4)
• *where 2 best of 4 scores count and a player plays off the wrong handicap in round 1, he is disqualified from that round but his scores may count in subsequent rounds* (D6.2b/5)
• *a player who plays off a higher handicap because he has failed to apply the USGA equitable stroke control provisions cannot be disqualified from a match* (DUS6.2a/100) *(applicable only in USA)*

Procedure

Penalty

Exceptions

h2   Handicap

Procedure

1 before starting a match players should determine their respective handicaps **(b)**

2 the applicable handicap is that current on the date of play (D6.2b/2)

b **should determine their respective handicaps**
- in foursomes a player mistakenly recorded his partner's handicap as 10 not 9 – both **disqualified** (D6.2b/2.5)

Penalty

disqualification – if a **higher** handicap is knowingly declared which would affect strokes given and received (R6.2a)

    no penalty – if a player plays off a **lower** handicap

Clearwater Bay GC, Hong Kong

What is it?

Basic rules

Exceptions

1 in *match play* failure to determine handicaps prior to the start of a match – **no penalty** (D6.2a/1)

2 when a handicap is wrongly calculated by the Committee and posted on a notice board by the Committee and a player wins off the wrong handicap – the competition result may be adjusted even several days later (D6.2b/3) – and the player's score adjusted according to his correct handicap Ⓒ

Ⓒ **application of the penalty**
• but when the Committee put a wrong handicap on the score card and the player played off a wrong handicap – **disqualified** *as correctness of handicap was his responsibility* (D6.2b/3.5)
• in match play by mistake a player took the wrong handicap and won – the result stood because he did not knowingly play off the wrong handicap – the onus was on his opponent to make a valid claim and this had not been done (D6.2a/5)
• in stroke play by mistake a player took the wrong handicap and won – this was not discovered until after the result had been posted – the result stood because he did not knowingly play off the wrong handicap and the error was not discovered within the prescribed time limit (D6.2b/1)

h3 HANDICAP ALLOWANCES

the customary allowances are:

Full allowance – Stroke play and Stableford competition

¾ of the difference – Match play, Fourball and Foursome competition

⅞ of the difference – Foursome variations

h4 | HANDICAP CERTIFICATE

What is it?

a certificate issued by a player's home club or golfing association as evidence of his current handicap

Procedure

1 players should carry one at all times and on visiting other courses they may be asked to produce the handicap certificate as evidence of their basic ability to play the game of golf

2 some courses will not admit players without handicap certificates – so it is advisable to check this requirement before visiting a golf club

h5 | HAZARD

What is it?

the general term for any bunker or water hazard or lateral water hazard (DF)
as rules and procedures vary for each different type of hazard see the detailed explanations under **Bunker** (see **(b33)**), **Lateral water hazard** (see **(l1)**) and **Water hazard** (see **(w2)**) as appropriate

What is it?

the general term for the area of play between and including the teeing ground and putting green

Basic rule

in a stipulated round the holes of the course must be played in the correct chronological order unless otherwise permitted by the Committee and it is the player's responsibility to know the correct order (D3/2)

Procedure

1 in *match play*:

(i) holes played in the wrong sequence are to be annulled **without penalty** and the match resumed at the proper hole (D2.3/4)

(ii) if a hole is omitted by mistake in a match and the mistake is not corrected the result still stands (D2.3/2) except both players will be **disqualified** if:

– the procedure unduly delays the competition (D2.3/4)

– a hole is omitted deliberately (D2.3/3)

2 in *stroke play* – players playing the holes out of sequence are **penalised 2 strokes** for playing from the wrong teeing ground under R11.4b (see **(t4)**) – and the error must be corrected before playing from the next teeing ground – if not – **disqualified** (D11.5/2)

What is it?

the term for the small sunken area on the putting green into which the ball must be struck to complete the play of each hole

Basic rules

1 in stroke play competition on a single day the Committee must ensure that all players play to the hole cut in the same position (R33.2b)

2 if the hole is badly damaged or surrounded by casual water it may be relocated as near as possible to the original position

3 if a hole is relocated otherwise than as above, the round should be declared void

4 in match play the hole may be relocated as necessary

5 a second hole cut on a double green is deemed **Ground under repair** (see **(g9)**) for players playing to the first hole and vice versa (D16/7)

Characteristics

it must be 4.25 inches/108mm diameter and at least 4 inches/100mm deep **(a)**. Any lining **(b)** must be sunk at least 1 inch/25mm below the surface of the putting green unless the nature of the soil makes it impracticable (DF)

a **at least 4 inches deep**
• hole cut on side of slope – should be sunk vertically even though the sides will be of different height (D16/6)

b **hole liner**
• hole liner not sunk 1 inch below the edge of the hole – players should draw to the attention of the Committee but not discontinue play *(D16/4)*
• hole liner pulled out with flag by accident – **no penalty** *(D17/7)*
• hole liner pulled out with flag by accident – ball strikes hole liner – **no penalty** – if hole liner moving – stroke to be replayed *(R19.1b)* if not, ball to be played as it lies *(R19.1)* *(D17/8)*

Procedure

① damage to the hole caused by a ball mark may be repaired **C** *(R16.1c)*

② repairing the ragged edge of a hole – **no penalty** if done as a courtesy but **2 stroke penalty** if done to influence the movement of the ball *(D1.2/3.5)*

C **repaired**
• if not, play should continue without repairing it unless its dimensions have been materially altered – if they have a player should request the Committee to repair it – if a Committee member is not readily available the player may repair it **without penalty** *(D16.1a/6)*

Paradise Island GC, Bahamas

What is it?

the term used to indicate that as a result of a stroke the ball is at rest within the circumference of the hole and all of it is below the lip  (a) (DF)

– see also *Ball overhanging the hole* (b19)

(a) **holing out**
• putt conceded under mistake of rules and the player moved to the next hole without holing out – **disqualified** (D3.2/1)
• ball blown into the hole by a player who then moved to the next hole without holing out with a club – **disqualified** (D3.2/2)
• ball embedded in the side of a hole and completely below the lip – deemed holed (R16/3)
NB if not completely below the lip – not deemed holed (D16/3)
• hole liner not properly inserted – ball struck liner and bounced out – not deemed holed (D16/5)

Basic rule

a ball must always be holed out in stroke play but need not be in match play as any stroke may be conceded

Procedure ➡

Penalty ➡

195

Procedure

(*stroke play* only) if a player fails to hole out he may correct his mistake before playing a stroke from the next teeing ground (or if at the last hole before leaving the putting green) – (R3.2)

Penalty

if the mistake is not corrected – **disqualified**

h8 HONOUR

the term to indicate which side or player is to play first from the teeing ground (DF)
for rules and procedures – see *Order of play* **(o4)**

Off the fairway at Milnerton GC, South Africa

manufactured ice is an **Obstruction** (see **(o3)**) (DF) natural ice
is either **Casual water** (see **(c4)**) or a **Loose impediment**
(see **(l9)**) at the option of the player (DF) see relevant entries
for applicable rules and procedures

i2 IDENTIFYING THE BALL

see also **Searching for the ball (s4)**

Basic rules

1 it is the player's
responsibility for playing
his proper ball and it is
recommended that he
put an identifying mark
on his ball (R12.2)

2 through the green a player may (provided he follows the
proper procedure) **without penalty** lift a ball he believes to
be his for the purpose of identifying it (a) and may clean
it but only to the extent necessary to identify it (R12.2)

3 on the green he may move, lift and clean it in any event

4 if a player cannot identify his ball within 5 minutes it is
deemed lost – see **Lost ball (l10)** for relevant rules and
procedures

Exception

the identification procedure
without penalty is **not**
permitted if the ball is in a
hazard – see **Searching for
the ball in a hazard (s4)** for
rules and procedure. It is
recommended that if there is
doubt as to the identification of
a player's ball in a hazard he
should attempt to play it as it
lies as there is **no penalty** if it
turns out to be the wrong ball

a identify
• ball lodged in a tree – player identified it with binoculars
but could not reach it – it is not a lost ball but an unplayable
ball (D27/14) – see **Ball unplayable (b23)**
• but if it is visible but not identifiable it is deemed lost (D27/15)
• if it cannot be identified because of mud – lift and clean it to
identify (D1.4/6)
• player with a ball identical to that of his fellow competitor lifted
it and changed to another ball to avoid confusion – **loss of
hole/2 stroke penalty** plus **1 stroke** for illegal lifting (D15/6.5)
• players playing identical balls hit both into
the rough – could not decide which is which
– as neither could identify his ball both are
lost balls (D27/10)
• but if a spectator could point out which
belonged to whom the balls are not
deemed lost (D27/12)

Procedure

Penalty

199

Procedure

when lifting a ball to identify it a player must:

(i) announce his intention of so doing

(ii) mark it

(iii) give his opponent or fellow competitor opportunity to observe the lifting and replacement

(iv) lift it and clean it to the extent permitted

(v) replace it

Penalty

for breach of procedures (i) – (iv) – **1 stroke** (R12.2) but for also failing to replace the ball the initial penalty is disregarded and there is a total penalty of **loss of hole/2 strokes** (R20.2a)

b **mark**

- *player who rotated the ball for the purpose of identifying it was* **penalised 1 stroke** *when he did not first mark it* (D12.2/2)
- *player who rotated the ball in a water hazard for the purpose of identifying it was* **penalised 1 stroke** *for moving it* (D12.2/3) – see **Ball moved – by player (b18)**

Basic rules

Exception

200

IGNORANCE OF THE RULES

Basic rule

ignorance of the rules does not warrant the mitigation of any
penalty nor the waiver of any procedure (a)

a **ignorance of the rules**
- *match discontinued because of darkness and the
players replayed the whole round instead of resuming where
they left off – result of replayed match stands (D2.3/5)*
- *ignorance of the rules does not invalidate the concession
of a hole wrongly given (D2.4/12)*
- *ignorance of the score does not invalidate the concession
of a match wrongly given (D2.4/14)*

ILLEGAL BALL

see *Ball – non-conforming* (**b6**)

ILLNESS

see *Discontinuance of play* (**d6**)

IMPEDIMENTS

see *Loose impediments* (**l9**)

IMPROVING LINE OF PLAY

see *Line of play* (**l7**)

INCORRECT INFORMATION

see *Wrong information* (w8)

INFLUENCING THE POSITION OR MOVEMENT OF THE BALL

What is it?

Examples include:

- catching the ball before it hits the bottom of the hole (D1.2/5)
- jumping on the green to try to make a moving ball fall in the hole (D1.2/4) **NB** stationary ball – **1 stroke penalty** only (R18-2a)
- loose impediment in a hazard removed by an opponent as a courtesy – thus improving a player's lie (D1.2/6)
- removing the flagstick from the green to avoid a ball hitting it (D1.2/3)
- shielding a ball from wind with a golf bag (D1.2/2)
- stepping on the line of an opponent's putt deliberately (D1.2/1)
- pressing down a tuft of grass on the line of a putt (D16.1a/17)
- repairing spike damage on the green (D13.2/36)
- positioning the flagstick anywhere other than in the centre of the hole (D17/4)
- opponent/fellow competitor picking up loose impediments on the green when requested not to do so by a player (D23.1/10)
- having a caddie hold back a tree branch to facilitate a drop procedure (D20.2a/5)

Basic rule

neither a player nor a caddie may take any action to influence the
position or movement of a ball unless permitted by the Rules (R1.2)

Exception

repairing damage to the edge of the hole as a courtesy –
no penalty (D1.2/3.5)

Penalty

loss of hole/2 strokes but **disqualification** for a serious
breach **(a)** (R1.2)

> **a** **serious breach**
> • *player deliberately stopped a
> putt from going in the hole* (D19.1/5)

*A player may not shield his ball from the wind with a golf bag or tap down
tufts of grass or spike marks on the line of his putt*

INJURY/ILLNESS

see *Discontinuance of play* (**d6**)

INSECTS

ant hills – are *Loose impediments* (see (**l9**)) but may also be declared *Ground under repair* (see (**g9**)) by the Committee (D33.8/22)

ants or bees etc on a ball – are *Loose impediments* (see (**l9**)) and may be removed **without penalty** (D23.1/5) unless the ball is in a bunker/hazard (D23.1/5.5)

bees nest – see *Danger* (**d1**)

INTEGRAL PART OF THE COURSE

What is it?

the technical term for constructions which do not qualify for relief as obstructions – as declared by the Committee under its powers to make local rules (R33.8) e.g. sides of bunkers, sides of teeing grounds sides of paths or roads etc.

Basic rule

as they are not obstructions there is no relief without penalty if the ball is against them or if they interfere with stance or area of intended swing

Procedure

1. play the ball as it lies or:

2. declare the **Ball unplayable** – see **(b23)**

Left: Hyatt Sanctuary Cove, Australia

What is it?

one from which it is impossible or impracticable (as deemed (a) by the Committee) to take relief by dropping a ball behind the hazard (b) on the extension of a line from the hole through the point where the ball last crossed the margin of the hazard.

The lateral part of the hazard is marked (c) with red stakes or a red line – stakes and lines are within the hazard (DF). The boundary extends vertically upwards and downwards

a   deemed
• *even though a hazard falls within the definition of a LWH the committee may still mark it as a water hazard if considered necessary to preserve the integrity of the hole (D26/3.5)*

b   behind the hazard
• *on the opposite side of the hazard from the hole (D26.1/15)*

c   marked
• *a ditch with one boundary out of bounds was marked not as a water hazard or a lateral water hazard – should be treated as lateral for relief purposes as it was not possible to drop a ball behind it (D26/3)*

Basic rules

Penalty

Procedure

Basic rules

1 if his ball lies in touches or is lost in a lateral water hazard a player is **under penalty** entitled to relief (R26.1) see Procedure

2 before making a stroke at a ball in or touching a lateral water hazard a player must not (R13.4):

(1) test the condition of the hazard or any similar hazard

(2) touch the ground in the hazard with a club or hand

(3) touch or move any loose impediment in or touching the hazard

EXCEPT

(a) the player may touch the ground

(i) as a result of or to prevent himself falling

(ii) in removing an obstruction

(iii) in measuring

(iv) in retrieving, lifting placing or replacing a ball under the Rules

(b) if the lie of a player's ball is affected by something after it came to rest (e.g. a divot from another player's stroke) the player may remove it **without penalty** as he is entitled to his original lie (D13.4/18)

3 stakes defining the boundary of the hazard are **Obstructions** (see **(o3)**) and may be moved **without penalty**

4 rules permitting lifting, cleaning and identifying the ball do not apply in a hazard (R12.2) **except** when searching for a ball in a hazard:

(i) in order to find the ball the player may probe with a club or otherwise

(ii) if the ball is covered by loose impediments – the player may remove by probing, raking or other means enough to see a part of the ball In both cases if any excess covering is removed and/or the ball moved ⓐ – **no penalty** but the ball must be replaced and if appropriate recovered so that only part is visible (R12.1) **unless** the player opts to take relief under procedure ❷ (ii), (iii) or (iv) (R12.1)

> ⓐ **moved**
> • player who rotated a ball in a water hazard for the purpose of identifying it **1 stroke penalty** under R18.2a (see **Ball moved (b18)** for touching it (D12.2/3)

Penalty

for breach of the rules – **loss of hole/2 strokes**

Procedure

Procedure

the player may either:

1 play the ball as it lies

or

2 lift and clean his ball and then take a **1 stroke penalty** and:

(i) play as near as possible from the spot where his previous stroke was played

or

(ii) drop a ball outside **(a)** the hazard within 2 club lengths of the point where the ball last crossed **(b)** the margin of the hazard provided it does not come to rest nearer the hole

or

(iii) drop a ball on the margin **(c)** of the hazard opposite to the point of entry within 2 club lengths of a point equidistant from the hole and coming to rest not nearer the hole

or

(iv) (iv) drop a ball any distance behind **(d)** the hazard but on the extension of a line from the hole through the point where the ball last crossed the margin of the hazard (NB this option should not be available as if this relief is possible its conflicts with the very definition of lateral water hazard - *author's note*)

What is it?

Basic rules

if the player has hit the ball from the tee into Dubai Creek, procedure option:

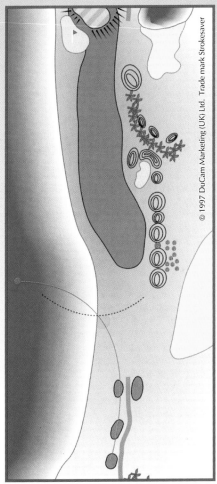

© 1997 DuCam Marketing (UK) Ltd. Trade mark Strokesaver

❷ (i) is available and requires him to take a **1 stroke penalty** and play his third stroke from the tee

❷ (ii) is available and requires him to take a **1 stroke penalty** and drop a ball within two club lengths of the point of entry but not nearer the hole – in the shaded area

❷ (iii) is not available as the opposite margin of Dubai Creek is not accessible from the course

17th Dubai Creek GC

Procedure

Penalty

a   outside the hazard
- means that the ball can be dropped on the same side of the hazard as the hole (D26.1/15)
- under 2(ii) if it is impossible to drop on the same side as the hole and not nearer it, a player must adopt one of the other options (D26.1/18)
- hazard was part water hazard and part lateral water hazard – ball crossed over the margin of the water hazard and ended in the lateral water hazard – since the ball never crossed the margin where it was defined as a lateral hazard option (ii) is not available so the only options are 2(i) and (iii) (D26.1/12)

b   last crossed
- player lost his ball in a lateral water hazard and took relief from the point where he believed the ball entered the hazard – the ball had in fact entered 20 yards away and was found in that position – as the player had not played his stroke he could redrop **without penalty** in the correct place under R20.6 – see **Wrong place (w9) NB** – if the player had already played from the wrong place – he should continue **without penalty** if his judgment was honestly made (D26.1/17)
- ball last crossed the margin of a hazard where it was marked as a water hazard but it came to rest in part marked as a lateral water hazard – must take relief as for water hazard NOT lateral water hazard (D26.1/12)
- where it is not possible to determine where it last crossed the margin only option 2(i) is available (D28/4.5)

c   opposite margin
- means any margin opposite the point of entry provided no land cuts a straight line between the point of entry and the equidistant point on the opposite side (D26.1/14)
- hazard was part water hazard and part lateral water hazard – the ball crossed the margin of the lateral water hazard and ended in the water hazard – player wanted relief under 2(ii) above – confirmed available as relief is determined according to the status of the hazard at the point where the ball last crossed a margin (D26.1/13)

What is it?

Basic rules

Procedure

d   behind
- behind may mean behind the point where the ball last crossed the margin of the hazard – not necessarily behind the entire hazard (D26.1/1.5)

Procedure (continued)

3 if a ball played from a lateral water hazard comes out of the hazard but is unplayable, lost or goes out of bounds the player may take a **further 1 stroke penalty** and:
(i) play as near as possible from the spot where the previous stroke was played from the hazard **or**
(ii) adopt Procedure **2** (ii) **or** **2** (iii) **or**
(iii) play as near as possible from the spot where the last stroke outside the hazard was played

4 if a ball played from a lateral water hazard remains in the hazard he may take a **1 stroke penalty** and in addition to the Procedure **2** options play as near as possible from where the last stroke outside the hazard was played

5 if pursuant to Procedure **3** or **4** the player opts to play from the spot where the previous stroke was played from the hazard he may elect not to play the dropped ball and take a **further penalty stroke** and adopt either **3** (ii) or (iii)

6 having chosen one of the relief options and proceeded under it a player cannot then change his mind and adopt one of the other options if the original is not satisfactory (R26.1)

7 if a player in a water hazard takes inappropriate relief as if for a lateral water hazard he is penalised **loss of hole/2 strokes** for playing from the *Wrong place* (see **(w9)**) plus in stroke play **a further 1 stroke** for breach of the *Water hazard* (see **(w2)**) procedure (D26.1/11) – he must then adopt the correct procedure – if not – **disqualified**

Penalty

Penalty

(f) breach of procedure – **loss of hole/2 stroke penalty**

(f) **application of the penalty**
• *serious breach of* R26 – *e.g. dropping 50 yards nearer the hole – the player must drop correctly and replay before playing from the next teeing ground as well as* **2 stroke penalty** – *if not* – **disqualified** (D26.1/21)

l₂ LEAVES

1. are *Loose impediments* (see **(l19)**) and may be removed **without penalty** except in a hazard. If in a bunker a player touches leaves with his backswing – **loss of hole/2 stroke penalty** (D13.4/33)

2. may also be *Ground under repair* (see **(g9)**) if so declared by the Committee

3. if they are knocked down from a tree during a practice swing it may be considered improving the *Area of intended swing* (see **(a11)**) – **loss of hole/2 stroke penalty** However, this is a matter of degree - knocking down a few leaves does not necessarily improve the area of intended swing

What is it?

the position in which the ball comes to rest on the course

Basic rules

1 a ball must be played as it lies unless the Rules provide otherwise (R13.1)

2 a player is entitled to his original lie so if this is made worse by subsequent events he will be entitled to recreate his original lie (a)

3 a player must not improve or allow to be improved the position or lie of his ball by moving bending or breaking anything growing or fixed including immovable obstructions and objects defining out of bounds or by removing or pressing down sand loose soil replaced divots (b) other cut turf placed in position or other irregularities of surface **except**

(i) as may occur in fairly (c) taking his stance

(ii) in making his stroke or the backward movement of his club for a stroke (d)

(iii) on the teeing ground in creating or eliminating irregularities of surface (e)

(iv) on the putting green in removing sand or loose soil or repairing damage as permitted by R16 – see **Putting green (p18)**

(v) in grounding the club which may only be done lightly and not so as to press it against the ground (R13.2)

(vi) after completion of the stroke – even if the player has then to take a drop on the spot where he has replaced/tapped down divots (D13.2/4.5)

a original lie
• lie affected by a pitch mark does not qualify for relief unless the pitch mark was made after the player's ball came to rest *(D13.2/8)*

• lie affected by sand when another player plays from a bunker – may remove the sand, lift and clean the ball as the player is entitled to a lie the same as when the ball came to rest *(D13.2/8.5)* a player is entitled to relief by recreating his original lie when his
– lie in a bunker is affected by another player's stroke *(D20.3b/1)*
– lie in a bunker is affected by another player's stance *(D20.3b/2)*
– lie is affected by removal of gallery control post *(D20.3b/3)*

b divot
• which is not completely detached is not a loose impediment and therefore cannot be removed or replaced even if it interferes with swing or lie *(D13.2/5)*

c fairly
• what is reasonably necessary without improving his situation but allowing a stance as normal as the circumstances permit e.g. a player may back into a branch even if it moves, bends or breaks – but may not deliberately move bend or break branches to get them out of the way of his backswing or stand on a branch to prevent it interfering with his swing or hook a branch against another to hold it back *(D13.2/1)*

d backswing
• sandy mound removed by backswing thus improving his lie – **no penalty** *(D13.2/9)*

e on the teeing ground
• even if done after an air shot i.e. when the ball is in play *(D13.2/2)*

Penalty

loss of hole/2 strokes

What is it?

i.e. picking it up and removing it from its position when it is in play
– see also **Ball interfering with play (b13)**, **Marking the ball
(m2)** and **Placing/replacing the ball (p8)**

Basic rules

1 (i) a player may lift his ball at any time (except if another ball
is in motion) **(a)** if he considers that leaving it in play will
assist another player (R22a). The ball may not be cleaned

(ii) a player may have any other ball lifted if he considers it
might interfere with his play or assist another player **(b)**
(R22b). In stroke play the other player may opt to play first
rather than lift his ball

2 a ball on the putting green may be lifted for any reason and
cleaned then replaced (R16.1b)

3 when play is discontinued before completing hole a ball may
be lifted and cleaned and should be marked so that on
resumption it can be replaced on its original spot (R6.8c) –
without penalty

4 a ball which has been lifted is **Equipment** (see **(e5)**) and also
an **Outside agency** (see **(o6)**) (D19.5/1 and 1.7)

5 a ball may be lifted when permitted by the Rules in order to
take relief – e.g from abnormal ground conditions etc **(c)**

Penalty

for lifting when not permitted – **1 stroke** provided the ball is
replaced (R18.2a) – see ***Ball moved by player (b18)***; for lifting
and failing to replace - **2 strokes** (D15/8)
for breach of Basic rule ❶ – **loss of hole/2 strokes**

a in motion
• if a ball on a putting green has been lifted and replaced it may
be lifted again if the player thinks a ball in motion may hit it (D16.1b/2)

b interfere or assist
• ball does not have to interfere physically with play – request
may be made if it catches another players eye and could distract him
D22/1)
• there must be a reasonable possibility that the ball will in some way
interfere (D22/3) – player who made several requests when there was
no reasonable possibility could himself be penalised under R6.7 – see
Delay (d3)
• there is no rule requiring a player who has lifted a ball under the rules
to replace it at the request of another player in order to assist his
play (D22/5)
• player may not request another not to lift his ball in order to assist his
play – if the player were to agree this would be deemed an agreement
to exclude rules – disqualification penalty under R1.3 (D22/6) – see
Agreement (a5)
• where a player did not opt to lift his ball which might assist other
players the Committee member watching the game was entitled
to intervene and request the player to lift
it to protect the player and the others
involved (D22/7)

c lifted
• once lifted a player may not change
his mind and not take relief from the
condition & supply replace the ball - if he
does **1 stroke penalty** (D18.2a/12.5)

Procedure

Penalty

Procedure

1. the ball may be lifted by the player, his partner or any other person authorised by him (a)

2. it may be necessary for the player to first announce his intention to lift e.g. if the ball is thought to be on an aeration hole, embedded, in a hole made by a burrowing animal, unfit for play or if he wishes to identify it.

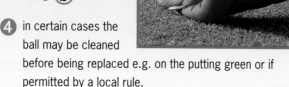

3. the position of the ball should be marked prior to lifting (b) (R20.1)

4. in certain cases the ball may be cleaned before being replaced e.g. on the putting green or if permitted by a local rule.

5. the ball must be replaced on the same spot after lifting – if not – **loss of hole/2 stroke penalty** (R20.1)

6. if the ball is accidentally (c) moved during lifting or marking– **no penalty** and replace (R20.1)

What is it?

Basic rules

Penalty

Penalty

for breach of procedure – **1 stroke**

a any other person authorised by him

- *opponent marked and lifted a player's ball without authority – the player then lifted the marker and claimed the hole – opponent **1 stroke penalty** – player **1 stroke penalty** for lifting marker – he must replace it and hole out (D20.1/3)*
- *opponent lifted a player's ball on the green without authority – opponent **1 stroke penalty** in match play (D20.1/2) – see **Ball moved (b18)***
- *fellow competitor lifted a player's ball on the green without authority – **no penalty** and the ball to be replaced – stroke play (R18.4) (D20.1/4) – see **Ball moved (b18)***
- *fellow competitor's caddie lifted a player's ball on the green without authority and then by mistake substituted another ball – **no penalty** as rule breach was a result of unauthorised lifting for which the player was not responsible – ball to be replaced (D20.1/5)*
- *if a player intends to lift a ball on the green but an opponent plays before the ball is lifted the opponent is **disqualified** for refusing to comply with a rule affecting the rights of another player (D3.4/1)*

b mark

- *player lifted his ball without marking it believing it to be a wrong ball – turned out to be his ball in play – **1 stroke penalty** for lifting without marking (D20.1/1)*

c accidentally

- *player dropped his putter on the ball whilst lifting it and moved it – **1 stroke penalty** because moving it was attributed to dropping the putter not lifting the ball (D20.1/14)*
- *player accidentally kicked the ball when stepping up to lift it – **1 stroke penalty** as movement of the ball was not attributable to the act of lifting (D20.1/13)*

l5 | LIGHTNING

for applicable rules see **Discontinuance of play (d6)**

Procedure

1 every precaution should be taken to protect players against lightning (App I)

2 players should be informed they have the right to stop play if they think lightning threatens them even though no official signal has been given

3 recommended signals – 3 siren notes to discontinue, 1 siren note to resume (App IV)

4 the Committee may provide that in a potentially dangerous situation play must be discontinued immediately on suspension of play (R6.8) – see **Discontinuance of play (d6)**

5 if the Committee orders resumption of play a player may refuse to continue **without penalty** if he believes he is still in danger (D6.8b/5)

l6 | LIMITED CLUB COMPETITION

a game under any format when the players are limited to the number of clubs they can carry and use for the round – often 2, 3 or 5 clubs. Otherwise all the rules of golf apply to the game

What is it?

the direction a player wishes his ball to take after a stroke plus a reasonable distance on either side. It extends vertically upwards but not beyond the hole (a) The term line of putt applies only when the ball is on the putting green

(a) **beyond**
• the hole itself is deemed to be part of the line of putt and may not be touched (D16.1a/5)

Preliminary

rules relate to doing any of the following to the line of play/putt:

(i)	improving it	(p224)
(ii)	indicating the line of it	(p226)
(iii)	standing astride it	(p228)
(iv)	repairing damage to it	(p229)
(v)	touching it	(p230)

Basic rules

(i) improving the line of play/putt

Basic rule

a player must not improve or allow to be improved his line of play
or a reasonable extension of that line beyond the hole by moving
bending or breaking anything growing or fixed including immovable
obstructions and objects defining out of bounds or by removing
or pressing down sand loose soil replaced divots other cut turf
placed in position or other irregularities of surface (R13.2) **(b)** or
by removing dew, frost or water

(b) examples
- *bunker raked by a player when his ball is outside it and the bunker is between his ball and the hole – **loss of hole/2 stroke penalty** (D13.2/28)*
- *moss or creepers in tree may not be removed to improve the line of play (D13.2/37)*
- *player whose ball is outside a bunker walks through the bunker to view his line to the green and then rakes out footprints before playing – **loss of hole/2 stroke penalty** because having worsened his line of play he cannot subsequently improve it (D13.2/29) but if he does the same pursuant to a rule (e.g. if he has taken a drop and it rolls into a bunker, he may rake the footprints and restore it to its original condition without penalty (D13.2/29.5)*
- *player removes a stone from a stone wall (immovable obstruction) to improve his line of play – **loss of hole/2 stroke penalty** (D13.2/32)*
- *player brushes away casual water on the putting green between his ball which is off the green and the hole – **loss of hole/2 stroke penalty** (D13.2/34)*
- *player brushes away dew/frost on the putting green between his ball and the hole – **loss of hole/2 stroke penalty** (D13.2/35) – unless it occurs incidentally to some other permitted action such as removing loose impediments*
- *player agrees to repair by fellow competitor of spike marks on his line of putt – both players **penalised 2 strokes** (D13.2/36)*

What is it?

Preliminary

Penalty

loss of hole/2 strokes

Exceptions

no penalty if:

1 the player improves his line of play

(i) in fairly taking his stance **C** (fairly see page 37)

(ii) in making his stroke or the backward movement of the club for a stroke

(iii) on the teeing ground in creating or eliminating irregularities of surface

(iv) on the putting green in removing sand or loose soil or repairing damage as permitted by R16

(v) in grounding the club which may only be done lightly and not so as to press it against the ground (R13.2)

2 a player improves his line of play incidental to taking relief under some other rule e.g. R25 when taking relief from abnormal ground conditions (R25.1b/3) – see **Burrowing animals (a10)**, **Ground under repair (g9)**, **Casual water (c4)** or when it occurs incidentally to some other permitted action e.g. removing **Loose impediments** (see **(l9)**) (D13.2/34) or **Moveable obstructions** (see **(o3)**)

3 the line of play is improved by an outside agency (e.g. spectator or greenkeeper) provided the player did not assist in or consent to the improvement (D13.2/33)

4 a player moves objects to the extent necessary to determine whether they are loose or attached provided if they are attached they are returned to their original position and the line of play/putt is not therefore improved (D13.2/26)

(ii) a indicating the line of play/putt When the player's ball is on the putting green

Basic rules

1 the player, his partner or either of their caddies may point out the line of putt but **only before and not during** the

stroke and provided the putting green is not touched (R8.2b)

2 in team competition the Committee may authorise each team to appoint and identify prior to him so doing one person e.g. team captain/coach who may give advice to members of that team – including advice as to the line of a putt (R8.2)

Procedure

1 a mark may not be placed to indicate the line of putt (a)

2 a player may not have the line of play indicated to him on the putting green by an opponent or fellow competitor (R8.2)

(a) **mark**
• placing a club on the ground to align the player's feet – **no penalty** provided it is removed before the stroke is played (D8.2a/1)

What is it?

Preliminary

Penalty

loss of hole/2 strokes

(ii) b indicating the line of play/putt When the player's ball is anywhere other than on the putting green

Basic rule

he may have the line of play indicated to him by anyone

Procedure

1. any mark to indicate the line of play during the play of a hole placed by the player or with his knowledge must be removed before the stroke is played (b)

2. touching the green to indicate the line of play when the ball is off the green – **no penalty**
(D8.2b/3)

b mark
- placing a club on the ground to align the player's feet – **no penalty** provided it is removed before the stroke is played (D8.2a/1)
- caddie casts a shadow to indicate the line of putt – **loss of hole/2 stroke penalty** if shadow is not removed before the stroke is played (D8.2b/1)
- placing a club off the line of play but at the point where he wants his pitch shot to land - loss of hole/2 stroke penalty (D8.2a/3)

Penalty

for breach of rule – **loss of hole/2 strokes**

(iii) standing astride the line of play/putt

Basic rules

1. nobody must stand on or near the line of play while a stroke is being played (EQ)

2. a player may not make a stroke from a stance astride or touching the line of putt or its extension behind the ball (R16.1e)

3. a player must not permit his caddie or partner to stand on or close to the line of play/putt or its extension behind ball **(a)** (R16.1f) when a stroke is being played anywhere on the course

a extension
• caddie stands off the green but on the extension of the line of putt – **loss of hole/2 stroke penalty** (D14.2/4) but not if the caddie was not there to assist the player e.g. if he was watching a player on another tee at the time of the putt (D16.1f/2)

Penalty

loss of hole/2 strokes

What is it?

Preliminary

Standing astride the line of putt is not permitted

(iv) repairing damage to the line of play/putt

Basic rules

1. hole plugs or ball marks on the green may be repaired (b)
without penalty – but not elsewhere (R16.1c)

2. spike marks on the line of putt or around the hole – cannot
be repaired (c) (D16.1c/4)

3. footprints or other indentations may not be repaired

(b) **may be repaired**
• *ball mark on line of a player's putt – he specifically requests
that another player does not repair it – must be left unless it also
affects the other player's line of putt – if repaired **loss of hole/2
strokes penalty** (D16.1c/2)*
• *ball mark is partially on and partially off the green – entire ball mark
may be repaired as it is not practical to repair only part of it (D16.1c/1.5)*

(c) **cannot be repaired**
• *even if done accidentally
during the course of legitimate
repair – **loss of hole/2 stroke
penalty** (D16.1a/16)*
• *spike marks in hole plug repaired
when repairing the hole plug – **no
penalty** (D16.1a/16.5)*
• *spike marks near a hole plug
repaired when repairing the hole
plug – **loss of hole/2 stroke
penalty** (D16.1a/16.5)*

Exceptions

Penalty

Spike marks cannot be repaired

l7   Line of play/putt

Exceptions

1. line of putt accidentally damaged by caddie's footprint – a player may ask the Committee to repair – if repair not possible it should be declared **Ground under repair** (see **(g9)**) and relief granted under R25.1b (D16.1a/13)

2. mushroom growing on the line of putt – relief as above (D16.1a/15)

3. line of putt deliberately stepped on by another player – footprint may be repaired prior to playing a stroke (D1.2/1)

Penalty

for illegal repair of line of play/putt – **loss of hole/2 strokes**

(v)   touching the line of putt

Basic rule

the line of a player's putt must not be touched (R16.1a) (a)

a   touched
• walking on the line of his own putt – **loss of hole/2 stroke penalty** against the player only if it was done deliberately (D16.1a/12) **no penalty** if another player accidentally walks on the line of putt (D16.1a/13)

What is it?

Preliminary

Exceptions

the line of putt may be touched **without penalty**:

1 to move sand loose soil and other loose impediments on the green by any means without pressing anything down (b)

2 in addressing the ball a player may place club in front of ball without pressing anything down

3 in measuring

4 in lifting and replacing the ball (c)

5 in pressing down a ball marker

6 in repairing old hole plugs or ball marks on the green

7 in removing moveable obstructions

A player may not brush aside loose impediments with a cap

(b) **examples**
   • may not brush aside or mop up casual water on the green (D16.1a/1) or dew or frost (D16.1a/3)
• removing an acorn was acceptable but then repairing the hole in which the acorn was embedded – **loss of hole/2 stroke penalty** (D16.1a/7)
• may not brush aside with cap or towel (D16.1a/8)
• a dozen strokes with palm of hand to remove small leaves was considered excessive – **loss of hole/2 stroke penalty** (D16.1a/9)

(c) **replacing**
   • habit of placing ball ahead of marker and rolling it back to the marker was not deemed touching the line of putt (D16.1a/17)

Penalty

for breach of rule – **loss of hole/2 strokes**

l8 LOCAL RULE

What is it?

a rule made by the Committee under R33 and Appendix 1 relating to abnormal conditions at the course for which the Committee is responsible. They are usually printed on the scorecard or if temporary handed out on the tee or in the pro shop

relate to (inter alia)

aeration holes	protection of young trees
boundaries and margins	roads and paths
dropping areas	sprinkler heads
environmentally sensitive areas	stones in bunkers
lifting a ball	temporary conditions
obstructions	water hazards
practice between holes	wet conditions
preferred lies	winter rules
preservation of the course	

Procedure

1. a player should always check the applicable local rules before starting his round

2. local rules may not waive the Rules of Golf (R33.8)

Penalty

for breach of local rule – **loss of hole/2 strokes**

What is it?

natural objects (a), provided they may be moved without unreasonable effort, delaying play and causing damage and provided they are not fixed, growing or solidly embedded (b) and do not adhere to the ball (c) (DF)

Examples

banana skin	detached divot (d)
half-eaten pear	aeration plugs
loose clod of earth	dung
a dead crab	a dead snake
leaves	fallen tree not attached to stump
branches	twigs
gravel on road (D23/14)	stones

sand and loose soil on the putting green – **but not** elsewhere

large stones only removable with difficulty (D23.1/2)

saliva (D25/6) but it may also be treated as casual water **(see c4)**

snow and natural ice can be loose impediments or casual water at the option of player

worms and insects plus casts or heaps made by them

worm half under the ground

but not dew and frost

a **natural objects**
• if transformed into something else e.g. logs into a table they are obstructions (D23/1)

b **solidly embedded**
• means not removable with ease (D23/2)

c **adhere**
• ball embedded in an orange – the orange is not a loose impediment as it was adhering to the ball – which must be played as it lies or declared unplayable (D23/10)

d divot

- divot which is not completely detached is not a loose impediment and therefore cannot be removed or replaced even if it interferes with the swing (D13.2/5)
- detached divot can be replaced but may not be pressed down if this would improve lie or area of intended swing (D13.2/6)
- divot need not be replaced in the hole from which it came (D13.2/7)
- divot from opponent's stroke came to rest adjacent to player's ball in bunker – he may remove it **without penalty** as he is entitled to his original lie (D13.4/18) **NB** – pine cone fell from tree and came to rest adjacent to a ball in a bunker – player could not move it as D13.4/18 only applies to the acts of a player, caddie or other animate outside agency (D13.4/18.5)

Leaves are loose impediments

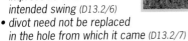

Basic rules

Procedure

Penalty

Exceptions

Basic rules

1 loose impediments may be moved (a) **without penalty** (R23.1) including from the area of drop (D23.1/6) or the area where a ball is to be placed (D23.1/6.5)

2 if the player moves his ball or causes it to move (b) whilst moving a loose impediment he incurs a **1 stroke penalty** and ball must be replaced (R18.2) – but **no penalty** if this occurs on the green (R23.1)

a   may be moved
- *loose impediments beyond the hole are left by a player but another player objects that they may assist play by stopping a ball rolling beyond the hole and requests that they be lifted – player need not lift them and the other player is* **penalised 1 stroke** *if he does so* (D23.1/10)
- *on top of a moveable obstruction can be moved with the obstruction* **without penalty** (D1.4/5)

b   moved
- *if a loose impediment is moved when a ball is lifted under the rules it must be replaced before the ball is replaced* (D23.1/7)
- *if a loose impediment is moved when a ball is lifted under the rules in order to prevent the ball moving when it is subsequently replaced –* **1 stroke penalty** *for circumventing R18.2 – see* **Ball moved (b18)** (D23.1/8) *– should remove the loose impediment before lifting or after replacing the ball*

What is it?

Procedure

1. loose impediments can be moved by any means unless on the line of putt when they can only be picked or brushed with the hand or club without pressing down (D23.1/1)

2. a player may obtain assistance to move a large loose impediment provided play is not unduly delayed (D23.1/3)

3. a player may break off part of a loose impediment such as a large branch rather than remove it (D23.1/4)

Penalty

for breach of rule – **loss of hole/2 strokes**

Loose soil is a loose impediment on the putting green....but not elsewhere

Exceptions

Exceptions

loose impediments may not be removed (R23.1)

1 when both the ball and the loose impediment lie in a hazard unless permitted by a local rule **a**

2 when the player's ball is moving

a   **in a hazard**
  • *loose impediment was accidentally moved in a bunker –* **no penalty** *provided the lie of the ball/area of swing/area of stance was not improved* (D13.4/13)

• *loose impediment deliberately moved in a bunker – player kicked a pine cone into a bunker and then picked it up and removed it –* **loss of hole/2 stroke penalty** (D13.4/14) *– if his ball also moves when he moves the loose impediment –* **no additional penalty** (D13.4/15)

• *loose impediment was removed from a water hazard but the player then decided not to play from the hazard but to drop a ball outside under R26.1 – still incurred* **loss of hole/2 stroke penalty** (D13.4/17)

• *loose impediment – partially embedded pine needle in bunker was touched during the backswing –* **loss of hole/2 stroke penalty** (D13.4/32)

• **no penalty** *if done during downswing as this is part of the stroke which is deemed to have commenced at the top of the backswing* (D13.4/33)

• *loose impediment which arrives in a hazard due to the action of another player or outside agency after his ball has stopped can be removed* **without penalty** *as he is entitled to his original lie e.g. stone kicked into bunker*

• *loose impediment on the line of play through a bunker may be moved if the ball is outside the bunker* (D13.2/31)

• *if both partners are in a bunker and one removes a loose impediments the other is only penalised if the act assisted his play* (D31.8/1)

10 LOST BALL

Preliminary

different rules apply according to whether it is lost:

(i) in casual water, ground under repair or in the hole/cast/runway of a bird, reptile or burrowing animal, when the problem area is:
(i) outside a hazard
(ii) within a hazard
p244

(ii) in a lateral water hazard p246

(iii) in a water hazard p248

(iv) anywhere else p249

Vilamoura II GC, Portugal

What is it?

Basic rules

Penalty

Procedure

Exceptions

What is it?

a ball is considered lost if (DF):

1 it is not found or identified a by the player within 5 minutes b of commencing the search for it a

or

2 the player has made a stroke at a substituted ball under the Rules before 5 minutes have elapsed and without announcing it as a provisional ball

or

3 the player has treated it as lost c by playing a provisional ball from where the original is likely to be or from a point nearer the hole d

but

4 a player cannot make a ball lost simply by declaring it to be so before the 5 minutes have passed

a identified

- *players playing identical balls hit both into the rough – if they cannot decide which is which – as neither could identify his ball both are lost balls (D27/10)*
- *but if a spectator could point out which belonged to whom the balls are not deemed lost (D27/12)*
- *ball lodged in tree – player identified it with binoculars but could not reach it – ball is not a lost ball but an unplayable ball (D27/14) – but if it is visible but not identifiable it is deemed lost (D27/15)*
- *player cannot find his ball and assumes it was removed by an outside agency so proceeds under R18.1 – see **Ball moved** (**b18**) – no evidence of outside agency so his procedure was wrong and he therefore played from a wrong place – **loss of hole/2 stroke penalty** and he must then proceed under the lost ball rules with an additional **1 stroke penalty** (D27.1/2.5)*
- *if found within 5 minutes it may be identified within a reasonable time outside the 5 minute period (D27/5.5)*

b 5 minutes
• time spent in playing a wrong ball is not counted in 5 minute search time (DF)

• time spent searching for a wrong ball is counted – player looked for 3 minutes and then found a ball which he played but it turned out to be a wrong ball – he is only allowed a further 2 minutes to find the correct ball (D27/2)

• original ball and provisional ball both hit into rough – player allowed 5 minutes if they are in the same area but 2 periods of 5 minutes if they cannot be searched for simultaneously (D27/4)

• player finds ball which he believes to be his opponent's – 5 minutes elapse without finding his own ball – he then discovers ball found was in fact his – must take **loss of hole/2 stroke penalty** as ball became lost ball after 5 minutes (D27/5)

• after 2 minutes a player declared his ball lost but when returning to the tee found his original ball – he could play it **without penalty** (D27/16)

• ball found after 5 minutes – not allowed to play it (D27/7)

• ball found after 5 minutes and played is a **Wrong ball (w7)** – **loss of hole/2 stroke penalty** plus in stroke play if the error is not corrected before playing from the next teeing ground – **disqualified** (D27/8)

• second ball teed but not played before 5 minutes has expired – the player then finds his original ball – **no penalty** because the teed ball is not in play (D27.1/1)

• second ball dropped but not played before 5 minutes has expired – the player then finds his original ball – **no penalty and original ball may be played** because a dropped ball is not in play (D27.1/2)

• searching longer than 5 minutes for a lost ball is undue delay – **loss of hole/2 stroke penalty** (D6.7/2)

• committee may intervene directly if undue delay (DUS34 3/101) (USA only)

c treated it as lost
• player plays a provisional ball believing that the original ball is lost and proposes to continue with the provisional – a Committee member knows where the original lies – he is obliged to advise the player and the player must continue with the original ball (D27.2/2)

d nearer the hole
• playing a provisional ball from where the original was last played and playing a second stroke with it when it is still further from the hole than where the original is believed to be lost is a proper procedure

Procedure

Penalty

Basic rules

Procedure

❶ a player cannot declare a ball lost in circumstances other than permitted by the Rules

❷ to save time if a ball may be lost <u>other than in a water hazard</u> a player should (but does not have to) play a provisional. If he does he should:

(i) inform his opponent/fellow competitor of his intention and
(ii) play a provisional ball from a spot as near as possible to where the original ball was played and before he or his opponent/fellow competitor goes forward to search for the ball (R27.2a) – for breach of (i) or (ii) **1 stroke penalty** and the provisional ball automatically becomes the ball in play
(iii) if the original ball is found the player should pick up his provisional ball and continue with his original ball under the relevant rules. If he continues with a provisional ball he is then playing a **Wrong ball** (see **(w7)**) – **loss of hole/2 stroke penalty** under R15 (R27.2c)
(iv) having played a provisional ball, once he reaches the spot where his lost ball is likely to be, if he plays a further stroke with the provisional ball it becomes the ball in play and the player incurs a **1 stroke penalty** (R27.2b)

❸ when a ball is lost, if the player drops another ball in the same area and continues with play – **loss of hole/2 stroke penalty** plus in stroke play a further **1 stroke penalty** and he must then play from where the original ball was previously played – if he does not rectify the breach and adopt proper procedure **disqualification** ⓐ (D27.1/3)

◀ **Preliminary**

◀ **What is it?**

242

④ it is advisable before commencing to search for a lost ball
for the player to announce the make and number of the ball
he is looking for – to avoid any disputes if a ball is found

⑤ if a search for a lost ball is delaying the group behind
players should allow that group to play through (EQ)

a adopt the proper procedure

• *player loses sight of his shot and believes it to
be in a bunker – he cannot find it and drops a second
ball in the bunker and plays it – the original ball is
then found behind the green – he should have
replayed from the place of the original shot; dropping
in the bunker was well in advance of the place of his
previous shot – serious breach so* **disqualified**
*(D20.7b/3) – provided he had not played from the next
teeing ground he should have gone back to the
original spot and replayed from there*
• *original ball lost so a provisional ball was played – the
original was then found, the second ball picked up and
the original ball played – the second ball was the ball in
play so the original ball became a wrong ball and for
playing it the* **penalty was loss of hole/2 strokes**
(D15/5)

Penalty

for breach of any of the lost ball rules – **loss of hole/2 strokes**

Basic rules

243

(i)   ball lost in abnormal ground conditions (a1)

Basic rules

1. Determine the point where the ball last entered (b) the abnormal ground condition

2. The ball is now deemed to be at this point

3. if the ball now lies through the green (t10): the player may take relief **without penalty** by dropping a ball within 1 club length (C) of the nearest point of relief being the point nearest to where the ball lies which avoids interference from the condition, is not nearer the hole and is not in a hazard or on a putting green (R25.1c(i))

4. if the ball now lies within a bunker: the player may take relief (i) **without penalty** by dropping a ball in the bunker within 1 club length of the nearest point of relief but if complete relief is not available as near as possible to the point where the original ball lies on ground affording maximum relief from the condition although not nearer the hole

   or

   (ii) **with 1 stroke penalty** by dropping a ball outside the bunker anywhere on the extension of the line between the hole and the point where the ball last crossed the margin of the hazard but not nearer the hole

Preliminary

What is it?

Procedure

Penalty

C   **club length**
• the ball is permitted to roll up to a further 2 club lengths – see **Club length (c11)**

⑤ If the ball now lies on the putting green place it **without penalty** at the nearest point of relief or if complete relief is impossible at a point which gives maximum relief - this may be off the putting green (R25.1c(iv))

⑥ there must be reasonable evidence ⓓ that the ball is lost in the problem area – if not and the player takes relief under these rules he is deemed to have played from the *Wrong place* (see **(w9)**) – **loss of hole/2 stroke penalty** and in stroke play he must adopt the general *Lost ball* procedure and take a **further 1 stroke penalty** and play from where the original ball was previously played; if the correct procedure is not adopted – **disqualified** (D25.1c/2)

⑦ Relief without penalty is not available if the ball now lies in a water hazard. The player must adopt the water/lateral water hazard procedures **(l1 and w2)**

ⓑ **entered**
• where the condition is casual water the ball is deemed to have entered where it last crossed the margin of the casual water (D25.1c/1.5)

ⓓ **reasonable evidence**
• there is no definition of this – it is a factual judgement to be made in this context of relevant circumstances in the particular case (D26.1/1)
• ball lands in casual water but the player cannot easily retrieve it – a ball is visible which may or may not be his – he must take relief as a lost ball unless the ball can be retrieved with reasonable effort (D25.1/1)
• player searched for 1 minute only and took lost ball relief – he subsequently found his original ball – if the search time was considered too short and therefore the presumption of loss not reasonable – the second ball was played from a wrong place – loss of hole in match play, **2 stroke penalty** plus adopt procedure ⑥ D26.1/3)

Basic rules

(ii) ball lost in a lateral water hazard

Basic rules

1 if the ball is lost in a **lateral water hazard** under **penalty of 1 stroke** the player may (R26.1):

(i) play a dropped ball as near as possible from the spot where the original ball was played

or

(ii) (C) drop a ball outside the hazard within 2 club lengths of the point where the original ball last crossed the margin of the hazard and not nearer the hole

or

(iii) drop a ball within 2 club lengths of a point on the opposite margin of the hazard opposite to the point of entry and equidistant from the hole (R26.1c)

2 if a ball played from a lateral water hazard comes out of the hazard but is lost again the player may take a **1 stroke penalty** and:

(i) drop as near as possible to the spot in the hazard where the original ball was played or **take a further 1 stroke penalty and**

Preliminary

(ii) adopt the Basic rule 1(ii) or (iii) procedure

or

What is it?

Basic rules

C **club length**
• *the ball is permitted to roll up to a further 2 club lengths – see **Club length (c11)***

Procedure

(iii) play as near as possible from the spot where the last stroke outside the hazard was played **NB** if player adopts ❷ (i) he may elect not to play the dropped ball and take a **further 1 stroke penalty** and adopt ❷ (ii) **or** (iii)

❸ there must be reasonable evidence (d) preponderantly in favour of the ball being lost in the hazard and that it is not lost elsewhere – otherwise lost ball rules under R27 apply – see **(l10 (iv))** (R26.1/D26.1/1)

where the player plays from the 53 yard marker into the lateral water hazard:

option ❶ (i) requires him to take the **1 stroke penalty** and play again from the 53 yard marker

option ❶ (ii) requires him to take the **1 stroke penalty** and play from within two club lengths of where the ball crossed the margin – in shaded area A

option ❶ (iii) requires him to take the **1 stroke penalty** and play from within two club lengths of a point equidistant from the hole to the point in ❶ (ii) but on the opposite margin – shaded area B

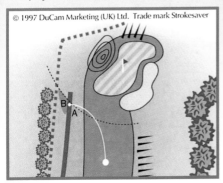

© 1997 DuCam Marketing (UK) Ltd. Trade mark Strokesaver

Left: 13th Brabazon Course, The Belfry, England

Basic rules

(iii) ball lost in water hazard

Basic rules

1 if the ball is lost in a water hazard under **penalty of 1 stroke** the player may (R26.1):

(i) play a dropped ball as near as possible from the spot where the original ball was played

or

(ii) drop a ball any distance behind the hazard on the extension of the line between the hole and the point where the ball last crossed the margin of the hazard

2 if a ball played from a water hazard comes out of the hazard but is lost the player may take a **1 stroke penalty** and (i) drop as near as possible to the spot in the hazard where the original ball was played or **take a further 1 stroke penalty** and:

(ii) drop a ball any distance behind the hazard on the extension of the line between the hole and the point where the ball last crossed the margin of the hazard **or**

(iii) play as near as possible from the spot where the last stroke outside the hazard was played

NB if player adopts **2** (i) he may elect not to play the dropped ball and take a **further 1 stroke penalty** and adopt **2** (ii) or (iii)

d **reasonable evidence**
• there is no definition of this – it is a factual judgement to be made in this context of relevant circumstances in the particular case (D26.1/1)

③ there must be reasonable evidence preponderantly in favour
of the ball being lost in the hazard and that it is not lost
elsewhere – ⓓ otherwise lost ball rules under R27 apply – see
Lost ball – (iv) Ball lost anywhere else (l10) (R26.1/D26.1/1)

(iv) ball lost anywhere else

Basic rule

if a ball is lost anywhere else the player must **under penalty
of 1 stroke** play another ball from a spot as near as possible
to where the original ball was played (R27.1)

Exceptions

① a ball believed lost but subsequently found in the hole is the
ball in play for score purposes even after search and playing
a provisional ball – **no penalty** (D1.1/2 and 3)

② a ball lost in an immoveable obstruction other than in a water
hazard – player may **without penalty** substitute another ball
and play it at the point where the original ball entered the
obstruction (R24.2c) and take relief as per the procedure for
Immoveable obstructions (see **(o3)**)
NB if lost in an immoveable obstruction where the entrance
is in a water hazard the player is not entitled to relief without
penalty and must proceed as for a water hazard **(W2)**.
Where the entrance is out of bounds it must be dropped
within 1 club length of the point where the pipe crossed the
OB line (D24.2b/12)

249

What is it?

a person appointed by the Committee ⓐ to record a competitor's score in stroke play competitions

> ⓐ **appointed by the Committee**
> • *if one is not appointed a lone player may appoint a third party to mark for him (D6.6a/1) if one is appointed marking by a third party is not acceptable (D6.6b/5)*

Procedure

① he may be a fellow competitor

② he is not a referee (DF)

③ he should check with the competitor and record his score after each hole ⓑ

④ he should sign the card after the round and hand it to the competitor ⓒ (R6.6a)

⑤ if more than one marker has marked the card each should sign for that part of the score for which he is responsible (R6.6a)

> ⓑ **record his score**
> • *marker who knowingly attests to a wrong score is deemed to have agreed to waive the rules – marker and competitor **disqualified** (D1.3/6) even though the competitor was unaware of the error (D6.6a/5)*
> • *refuses to sign the card because of a dispute – Committee upholds the player's view – the marker still refuses to sign – the marker is entitled to refuse provided he has told the Committee of his objection – the Committee should accept certification from anyone who witnessed play; if nobody witnessed it, then they should accept the player's own account (D6.6a/4)*

MARKER (2)

What is it?

a small coin or similar item used to mark the position of the ball prior to lifting the ball when so permitted by the Rules

– see **Marking the ball (m1)** for applicable rules and procedure
– see **Ball interfering with play (b13)** for rules where the marker interferes with play

Stellenbosch GC, South Africa

C **hand the card to the competitor**
• *marker leaves the course with the competitors card – Committee should attempt to find him; if unsuccessful they should accept attestation of anyone who witnessed the round; if nobody did then they should accept the attestation of the player (D6.6b/6)*

253

What is it?

the procedure for identifying the exact position of the ball before moving it so that it can subsequently be replaced in that same position – see also **Lifting the ball (l14)** and **Placing the ball (p8)**

Basic rules

1 when permitted by the Rules the position of the ball should be marked by placing a ball marker, small coin or similar immediately behind it **(a)** (R20.1)

2 a ball marker is a moveable **Obstruction** (see **(o3)**) so it can be moved **without penalty (b)** (D24.1/5)

3 it is not a player's equipment so a ball deflected by it must be played as it lies (D20.1/17)

a **immediately behind**
• marking a ball 2 inches behind it – **1 stroke penalty** (D20.1/20)
• marking ball by reference to a blemish on the green and not putting down a marker – **1 stroke penalty** (D20.1/16)
• ball a marked by placing the toe of the club behind it – **no penalty** (D20.1/16)
• ball marked by daisy – acceptable (D20.1/16)
• ball marked by scratching a line with a tee – **no penalty** as long as it is not deemed testing the surface but this is discouraged because of possible damage to green (D20.1/16)

Marking two inches behind the ball is not permitted

b moved

- player dropped the marker on the ball whilst lifting and moved it – **1 stroke penalty** because movement was attributed to dropping the marker not to marking the ball (D20.1/15)
- marker accidentally stuck to the sole of player's shoe so he could not determine where to replace the ball – as the marker was not

moved during the process of marking or lifting – **1 stroke penalty** and ball to be replaced as near as possible (D20.1/5.5)

- marker stuck to sole of putter during process of marking – **no penalty** (D20.1/6)
- player placed finger on marker whilst brushing away loose impediments on green. Marker stuck to finger when lifting – **no penalty** as touching marker is deemed extension of marking process (D20.1/12)
- marker accidentally kicked away by player's caddie – **1 stroke penalty** (D20.1/7)
- marker picked up in mistaken belief that the hole was won – **1 stroke penalty** and replace the ball as near as possible to the original spot (D20.1/8)
- marker picked up by an outside agency – **no penalty** and replace (D20.1/9)
- marker blown off the green by wind or moved by casual water– **no penalty** and replace (D20.1/10)
- marker in a position to assist an opponent is moved by player – opponent cannot insist that it be left (D20.1/11)

Procedure

Penalty

Procedure

1 the player or anyone authorised by him may mark the ball

2 if the marker interferes with the line of play, stance or stroke of another player – on request it should be moved one or more clubhead lengths to one side (R20.1)

3 if the ball is moved accidentally during the process of marking – **no penalty** and replace it **C** (D20.3a/1)

4 marking behind the ball is recommended, but to the side or in front is permissible – **NB** in front may be deemed influencing the movement of the ball if the grass is pressed down (D20.1/19)

C accidentally
• *player marked his ball before moving an obstruction then replaced it but the ball moved when the marker was removed* – **no penalty** (D24.1/5)
• *ball marked and then knocked aside as opposed to lifted* – **no penalty** (D20.1/22)
• *player accidentally kicked the ball when stepping up to lift it* – **1 stroke penalty** *as movement of the ball was not attributable to the act of lifting* (D20.1/13)

What is it?

Basic rules

Penalty

for breach of procedure **1 stroke**

MATCH PLAY

a game scored by holes rather than strokes (R2.1)

Basic rules

1 holes are scored by the lowest number of strokes and scoring in the match is reckoned by 'holes up', 'all square' and 'holes to play' (R2.1)

2 stroke play and match play competitions cannot be played simultaneously – if they are – results should be disregarded by the Committee (R33.1)

MEDAL PLAY

see **Stroke play (s29)**

Port Royal GC, Bermuda

MOVING BALL

see *Ball deflected (b8)* for applicable rules and procedures

Basic rule

a player must not play the ball whilst it is moving (R14.5)

Penalty

loss of hole/2 strokes

Exception

no penalty for playing a moving ball in a water hazard

 MUD

if on the course – see *Casual water (c4)*
                        Ground under repair (g9)

if on the ball   – see *Cleaning the ball (c8)*
                        Identifying the ball (i2)

 MULLIGAN

the practice of allowing the first tee shot to be replayed **without penalty** if it proves unsatisfactory, is **NOT** recognised in the rules of golf

MULTIPLE BREACHES OF RULES

What is it?

(1) When prior to playing a stroke a player

(i) breaches one rule more than once either by one act (e.g. when putting on the green he hits 2 other balls belonging to other players) or by repeating (a) the same/similar acts (e.g. playing several practice strokes in a bunker and touching the sand each time)

(ii) breaches two rules either by one act (e.g. when putting from a bunker he rakes a footprint on his line of play – he is deemed testing the condition and improving his line of play) or by repeating the same/similar acts (e.g. putting from the fairway he removes sand on his line of play and also presses down a divot on his line of putt)

(2) When prior to playing a stroke a player

(i) breaches one or more than one rule by different acts (e.g. when putting on the green he lifts his ball without marking it and then touches his line of putt)

Penalty

for (1)(i) and (1)(ii) – only one **penalty** (b) is incurred in total

for (2)(i) – one **penalty** (b) is incurred for each breach

(a) repeating
• if he has been told that his action constitutes a breach of the rules and he continues to touch the sand with practice swings he incurs separate penalties for each breach (D1.4/13)
• if in practising he touches the sand before the stroke and then fails to get the ball out of the bunker and practices again – again touching the sand – he incurs separate penalties for each breach (D1.4/14)

(b) one penalty
• if the player breaches two rules having different penalties, the more severe penalty will apply (D1.4/15)

n1 NASSAU

a game where a player or side scores 1 point for winning the first 9 holes, 1 point for the second 9 and a further point for winning the overall 18 holes. There will be 2 separate games being played at any one time – the 18 hole game plus a 9 hole game (a)

a **scoring**
• *player who won the first 9 but withdrew from second 9 due to illness still scored 1 point but lost the second 9 and overall match by default* (DUS2.3/100) *(applicable in USA only)*

n2 NEAREST POINT OF RELIEF

The reference point for relief from a wrong putting green, **(p18)** an immoveable obstruction **(o3)** and from abnormal ground conditions **(a1)** caused by burrowing animals, casual water and ground under repair

It is the point on the course nearest to the ball which avoids interference by the conditions and is not nearer the hole.

If it cannot be determined precisely it should be estimated (D24.2b/2.5)

In determining the point the player must use the club, form of address and intended swing he would have used had the problem condition not been there (D24.2b/1)

Left: Boyne Highlands GC, Michigan

01 | **O. B.**

abbreviation for *Out of bounds* (see **(05)**)

02 | **OBSERVER**

What is it?

a person appointed by the Committee to assist a referee to decide questions of fact and to report to him any breach of the Rules (DF)

Procedure

he should not:

① attend the flagstick – but **no penalty** if he does (D17.1/3)

② stand at or mark the position of the hole

③ lift or mark the position of the ball – but he may do so if specifically authorised by the player (R20.1)

Above: Vale de Pinta GC Portugal
Left: Jasper Park GC, Canada

263

What is it?

anything artificial unless it has been declared an **Integral part of the course** (see **(i12)**). For rules purposes obstructions are deemed either:

| **1** | moveable obstructions | (page 266) |

| **2** | immoveable obstructions (DF) | (page 268) |

for rules and procedures re natural objects see **Loose impediments (l9)**

Examples

- abandoned ball (D24.1/2)
- ball marker (D24.1/5)
- bridge – ball on bridge over deep hollow – must drop within one club length of the point vertically beneath the ball (D24.2b/11)
  NB no relief if the bridge is over a water hazard
- car park (D24/10)
- cart path – if artificially surfaced (D24/9)
- clubhouse is an immoveable obstruction – some parts may be moveable e.g. doors and windows – player who hit ball into clubhouse could open window to play it out again (D24.2b/14)
- drainage hose is moveable obstruction (D24.2b/15.3) underground drainpipe – must drop within 1 club length of the point vertically above where the ball came to rest in the pipe the ball (D24.2b/12)
- fence which leans over into the course – provided it is not a boundary fence (D13.2/20)
- gate in boundary fence/wall – may be closed if it interferes with a player's swing (D27/18)
- manufactured ice
- parked car can be moveable or immoveable according to the circumstances (D24/8)
- path if artificially surfaced (D24/9)
- rake
- road if artificially surfaced

- stile attached to boundary fence unless the Committee has declared it to be part of the course (D24/1)
- surfaces and sides of roads and paths if artificial
- sprinkler head
- supports or guy wires for boundary fence (D24/2)
- stakes defining lateral water hazards and water hazards
- stone broken away from retaining wall in hazard – the stone is a moveable obstruction and the player entitled to relief but the wall is immoveable and therefore no relief because it is in a water hazard (D24/6)
- stone covering entrance to drain in bunker to prevent sand draining away is part of drain and therefore an immoveable obstruction (D24/7)
- wooden planks (D24/11)
- wooden steps cut into bank (D24/12) but not uncovered steps cut into soil (D24/12)

but not
- objects defining out of bounds (e.g. walls, fences, stakes, railings) (a)
- any part of an immovable object which is out of bounds
- any construction declared by the Committee to be an integral part of the course (DF)
- concrete bases for boundary fence posts (D24/3)
- line drawn on ground for crowd control (D24.2b/20)
- immoveable objects situated out of bounds (D24.2b/21)
- internal out of bounds posts unless otherwise declared by the Committee (D24/5)
- turf covering an underground but raised pipe (D24/14)
- paths/roads which do not have an artificial surface
- stones in bunkers unless authorised by a local rule

Basic rules

(a) **out of bounds**
• ball simultaneously against a boundary fence and an immoveable obstruction – the player is entitled to relief even though it effectively gives him relief from the boundary fence (D24.2b/6)

Penalty

Procedure

1 moveable obstructions (b)

Basic rules

a player is entitled to relief **without penalty** (R24.1)

1 **if his ball is *not* in or on the obstruction** – by removing the obstruction. If the ball moves because of removal of the obstruction it must be replaced **without penalty**

2 **if his ball *is* in or on the obstruction** – by lifting the ball and then removing the obstruction – the ball should then be dropped (or on the putting green placed) as near as possible to where it lay but not nearer the hole

3 if they interfere with his stance or area of intended swing – see **Area of intended swing (a11)** for rules and procedures

Penalty

for breach of the rule – **loss of hole/2 strokes** (c)

 application of penalty
• *wrongly taking relief by moving a boundary post – even if the error is realised and the post replaced before the stroke is played –* **loss of hole/2 stroke penalty** (D13.2/25)

What is it?

b **moveable**
 • *it is moveable if it can be moved without unreasonable
effort, without delaying play and without causing damage (DF)*

Procedure

1 except as in Rule **2** a player cannot touch his ball to prevent
   it moving whilst moving the obstruction – this would be
   breach of R18.2a – see ***Ball moved (b18)*** (D24.1/4)

2 when a ball is moving an obstruction which is in its path and
   which may interfere with its movement may not be removed
   (except an attended flagstick)

3 an opponent/fellow competitor incurs the **loss of hole/2
   stroke penalty** if he moves an obstruction when the player
   has requested him to leave it (D24/16)

4 a player can move a moveable obstruction which interferes
   with his stance or ***Area of intended swing*** (see **(a11)**)

2 immoveable obstructions

Basic rules

when a ball lies in, on or so close to an immoveable obstruction that it interferes (C) with a player's stance or area of intended swing (d) (**NB** not if it is merely on his line of play except for Exception 6) he may obtain relief **without penalty** by (R24.2b):

1 **through the green/on the teeing ground** – lifting the ball and dropping it within one club length (e) of the nearest point of relief being the point on the course nearest to where the ball lay (f) provided:
(i) it is not nearer the hole
(ii) it is not in a hazard or on the putting green
(iii) it avoids interference from the obstruction

2 **in a bunker** – **without penalty** lift and drop as above but within the bunker or **1 stroke penalty** and drop outside and behind the bunker on the extension of the line from the hole through the spot where the ball originally lay in the bunker'(R24.2b(ii))

3 **on the putting green** – lift and place as above but on the green. Relief from interference with the line of putt is available if both ball and obstruction are on the green – see **Line of play/putt (l17)**

4 **ball lost in an immoveable obstruction** - see **Lost ball (l10)**

A sprinkler head is an immoveable obstruction

What is it?

C interferes
• *must be physical interference not just a distraction that diverts his attention (D24.2a/1)*

d area of intended swing
• *in the direction he would have played if the obstruction had not been there (D24.2a/2)*

e one club length
• *in determining both the point of relief from an immoveable obstruction and whether interference continues to exist the player should measure with the club he intends to use for the next stroke. If there is still interference he must redrop even though he could avoid the interference by using a different club (D20.2c/0.7). Having redropped he may use a different club to play his next stroke (D24.2b/4)*

*If the bridge is over a hollow the player must drop the ball in the hollow. If it is over a water hazard – no relief – he must play it as it lies or take relief from the water hazard under penalty see **Water Hazard (w2)***

f nearest point
• *immovable obstruction in ground under repair interferes with swing – the player may drop in ground under repair and then take further relief from the ground under repair – see **Ground under repair (g9)** (D24.2b/10)*

Procedure ➤

Exceptions ➤

Penalty ➤

Procedure

1 the player should mark the point on the course where he proposes to take the drop

2 in taking relief from an immoveable obstruction when the ball is in the rough the player may drop on the fairway as there is no distinction between rough and fairway in 'through the green' (D24.2b/8)

3 if in taking relief from the obstruction the player encounters a further obstruction he is entitled to relief again (24.2b/9)

4 in judging where interference would cease to exist the club which the player would expect to play next must be used (D24.2b/4) – but having dropped the ball he may use another club to play the stroke

5 if the ball is not recoverable from an immovable obstruction another ball may be substituted **without penalty** (R24.2b)

6 an opponent/fellow competitor incurs a **loss of hole/2 stroke penalty** if he moves an obstruction when the player has requested him to leave it (D24/16)

h **anything other**
• *ball unplayable because of tree roots but the area of swing is also impeded by an immoveable obstruction – **no relief** (D24.2b/16)*
• *right handed player playing left handed to avoid a boundary fence is not an abnormal stance – entitled to relief when the obstruction interferes with his stance (D24.2b/17)*
• *NB right handed player playing left handed to improve his position even though he could have played right handed is an abnormal stance – **no relief** when the obstruction interferes with his left handed stance (D24.2b/17)*

What is it?

Basic rule

Exceptions

1. **no relief** if the obstruction is in a water hazard – he must play the ball as it lies or proceed under R26.1 – see **Lateral water hazard (l1)** or **Water hazard (w2)**

2. **no relief** if the interference is with an unusually abnormal stance, area of swing or direction of play (R24.2b)

3. **no relief** if the interference is also by anything other than the immoveable obstruction which would render it unreasonable for the stroke to be played (h)

4. **no relief** if it merely interferes with the line of play other than on the putting green

5. **no relief** if the obstruction is out of bounds

6. the local rules of the course may provide for special relief including relief if they are on the line of play from sprinkler heads lying within 2 club lengths of the putting green (R33.8/App 1). Check the local rules on the scorecard

Penalty

1. wrongly taking relief in the belief that an object is an obstruction e.g. dropping away from boundary wall – **1 stroke penalty** under R18.2 – see **Ball moved – by player (b18)**

2. for breach of rules or procedure **loss of hole/2 strokes**

Procedure

1 from the **first teeing ground**:

(i) the person or side to play first (i.e. having the honour) should be decided by draw or if no draw, by lot

(ii) in informal games it is a common practice, but not one contained in the Rules, to tee off in the order of ascending handicaps

(iii) it is also a common practice, but not one contained in the Rules, for men to tee off before women as this tends to assist the pace of play by virtue of the position of their respective teeing grounds

2 from **subsequent teeing grounds**:

• in match play the person or side which wins the previous hole has the honour. If a hole is halved the side which had the honour retains it (R10.1a)

• in stroke play – the competitor with the lowest gross score at the previous hole has the honour and others play in ascending order. If equal scores they play in the same order as at the previous tee (R10.2a and D10.2a/1)

• in Stableford – the player with the best net score at the previous hole has the honour

• a provisional/second ball from the teeing ground must be played after an opponent/fellow competitor has played his first stroke (R10.3)

3 **elsewhere** – the ball farther/farthest from the hole should be played first; if equidistant, decide by lot ⓐ (R10.1b and 2b)

Penalty

for playing out of turn:

in match play an opponent can require the offender to cancel the stroke and replay the ball as near as possible from the original spot (R10.1c)

in stroke play – **no penalty** (b) unless the Committee decides it was done to give the player an advantage – in which case – **disqualification** (R10.2c)

(b) **application of penalty**
  • *playing out of turn by agreement in stroke play is not deemed an agreement to waive the rules so **no disqualification penalty*** (D10.2c/2)
  • *player plays out of order – realises his mistake – abandons the first ball and plays a second ball in the correct order – the first ball is deemed a lost ball – **1 stroke penalty*** (D10.2c/1)

Exceptions

see *Foursomes* (**f10**) and *Threesomes* (**t9**)

(a) **equidistant**
  • *in deciding distances approximate judgments are accepted* (D10.1b/1)
  • *if both balls are in a hazard order is decided by their relative positions before relief is taken* (D10/1)
  • *if both balls are lost in a hazard order should be decided by lot* (D10/3)
  • *in deciding distances in order to determine the order of play players may ask the distance of their respective balls from the hole – although this is not recommended as it is in theory deemed giving* **advice (a3)** (D8.1/2.5)

What is it?

ground beyond the boundaries of the course or any part of the course appropriately marked. It is usually marked by white posts/stakes or a white line. When defined by stakes or a fence it is the line between the nearest inside points at ground level excluding angled supports (a). When it is a line the line itself is out of bounds and is deemed to extend vertically upwards and downwards (DF)

a **nearest inside points**
• *if a fence is supported by vertical posts on the course side the OB line is the line of the nearest inside points of the posts (D27/19)*

Basic rules

1. if a ball is out of bounds (b) the player incurs a **1 stroke penalty** and must play a ball as near as possible from the spot from which the original ball was played (R27.1)

2. posts defining out of bounds are not obstructions and a player is therefore generally not entitled to relief from them either if his ball is close to them or if they interfere with his area of intended swing. To take relief he would have to declare his ball unplayable and incur a **1 stroke penalty** – see **Ball unplayable (b23)**

b **out of bounds**
• *all of the ball must be out to be deemed OB (DF)*

The player may stand out
of bounds to play a ball
which is in bounds

if all of the ball is on or over the line it is out
of bounds

Procedure →

Penalty →

Procedure

1 if the original ball was played
   – from the teeing ground the replayed ball may be teed
   – through the green it must be dropped
   – from the putting green it must be placed (R20.1)

2 the player may stand out of bounds to play a ball which is
   in bounds

3 if a player plays a ball which is out of bounds – as it is not
   the ball in play it becomes a wrong ball – **loss of hole/2
   stroke penalty** (D15/6) and he **must** also adopt the out of
   bounds procedure and incur a **further 1 stroke penalty**
   as above

Exceptions

a ball may not be played from the spot from which the original ball
was played if it is out of bounds
(i) in a water hazard – proceed under water hazard rules – see **L1**
and **W2**
(ii) in abnormal ground conditions - proceed appropriately – see
animals a10, **casual waterc4** or **ground under repair g9**

What is it?

Basic rule

Penalty

for not playing from the spot from which the ball was previously
played – **loss of hole/2 strokes** (C)

NB if in stroke play he plays from a wrong place he may also be
disqualified (C) – see *Wrong place* **(w9)**

(C) **application of penalty**
- *ball hit out of bounds was thrown back in by outside
agency who informed a caddie but the caddie did not tell the
player – the ball became a **Wrong ball** (see **(w9)**) and the **loss
of hole/2 stroke penalty** applied (D15/9) if neither the player
nor the caddie knew – **no penalty** (D15/10)*
- *player's ball hit a maintenance vehicle and went out of bounds –
the player dropped his ball back in bounds by the vehicle – **2
stroke penalty** for breach of the out of bounds rule plus a
further 1 stroke and distance penalty to comply with the out
of bounds procedure (D20.7/1) – but if the breach was serious –
i.e. he played from much nearer the hole – **disqualified***

06 OUTSIDE AGENCY

anything which is not part of the match e.g. referee, marker,
observer, caddie, ball which is not in play, ball from another
group, maintenance vehicle, spectator, power line, marker post,
live animal
(**NB** not wind or water) (DF)
for relevant rules and procedures see *Ball moved* **(b18)**,
Ball deflected **(b8)**, *Lost ball* **(l10)** or *Out of bounds* **(o5)**
as appropriate

p

P1   PAR

the score which an expert golfer would be expected to make at
any hole and allowing two strokes for putting – yardages are
arbitrary and allowance should be made for severity of ground and
unusual conditions

	men	**women**
par 3	up to 250 yards	up to 210 yards
par 4	470	400
par 5	over 471	575
par 6	over 576	

P2   PAR COMPETITION

a game in which play is against a fixed score at each hole (called
the par or bogey) – it is scored as in match play with plus 1 if the
player scores better than the par, equal if he scores par and
minus 1 if more than par. The winner is the player with the highest
aggregate score (R32.1a)

P3   PARTNER

a player on the same side (DF)

may be an obstruction. A player is usually only entitled to relief if it interferes with his stance, area of intended swing or his ball is on it if it is artificially surfaced. An unsurfaced footpath or road does not usually qualify for relief unless it is so provided in the local rules of the course or it has been defined as **Ground under repair** (see **(g9)**) – see also **Obstruction – immoveable (o3)** and **Area of intended swing (a11)**

Cart paths at Plantation GC, Amelia Island, Florida

Types ❶ disqualification

the penalty for the most serious breaches of the Rules. In match play disqualification may apply either to the hole being played or to the match itself *(see relevant alphabetical entry for full explanations)* it is the prescribed penalty for the following offences:

agreement – to play out of turn and thereby secure an advantage (R10.2 – stroke play only)

– to waive any rule or penalty (R1.3)

artificial device – using (R14.3)

ball – using non conforming (R5.1)

– applying 'foreign material' to (R5.2)

ball deflected or stopped – deliberately (R1.2)

caddie – having more than one at any one time (R6.4)

club – deliberately changing playing characteristics of (R4.2)

– applying 'foreign material' to the face of (R4.3)

– failing to declare excess out of play (R4.4)

delay – unduly delaying play* (R6.7)

discontinuing play – without committee approval (R6.8 – stroke play only)

etiquette – persistent serious breaches

foursome – playing out of turn and not subsequently correcting the error (R29)

handicap – failing to record on scorecard (R6.2 – stroke play only)

– declaring a higher handicap (R6.2)

hole out – playing from the next tee without holing out on the previous green (R3.2 – stroke play only)

holes – not playing in the correct order (R1.1 – stroke play only)

influencing position or movement of the ball – deliberately (R1.2)

practising – on course on day of play (R7.1 – stroke play only)

rules – refusing to comply with a rule affecting the rights of
   another player (R3.4)

score card – failing to sign (R6.5)
   – failing to have marker sign (R6.5)
   – signing incomplete or incorrect (R6.6)

second ball – playing and not subsequently reporting
   circumstances to the committee (R3.3)

teeing ground – playing from outside and not subsequently
   correcting the error (R11.4 – stroke play only)

tee markers – deliberately moving them (R11.1)

tee time – failing to start at the appointed time* (R6.3)

threesome – playing out of turn and not subsequently correcting
   the error (R29)

unusual equipment – using (R14.3)

wrong ball – playing and not subsequently correcting the
   error (R15.3) stroke play only

wrong place – playing from and not subsequently correcting the
   error (R20.7) stroke play only

Types ➋ 2 strokes

the usual penalty in stroke play unless otherwise provided in the
Rules (R3.5)

Types

Basic rules

Procedure

283

Types ❸ loss of hole

the usual penalty in match play

Types ❹ 1 stroke penalty

It is the prescribed penalty for the following offences
(see relevant alphabetical entry for full explanations)

address – player causes ball to move after (R18.2)

ball (stationary) moved – by an opponent, his caddie or
  equipment in match play (R18.3)

  – by a player, his caddie or equipment (R18.2)

ball overhanging hole – drops in after 10 seconds (R16.2)

ball struck more than once (R14.4)

ball unplayable – taking relief when (R28)

ball unfit for play – not announcing intention to lift to inspect to
  determine (R5.3)

casual water – taking relief from casual water in a hazard by
  dropping the ball outside (R25.1)

cleaning a ball – when not permitted (R21)

delay – for first offence if tournament rules so provide
  (if not – **disqualification**) (R6.7)

dropping the ball – in an incorrect manner (R20.2)

  – so that it lands nearer the hole

  – failing to do so when required by the rules (R20.2)

ground under repair – taking relief from g.u.r. in hazard by
  dropping ball outside (R25.1)

hazard – taking relief from by dropping the ball outside (R26.1)

Types

identifying the ball – adopting incorrect procedure (R12.2)
  – lifting ball from a hazard to identify (R12.2)
lateral water hazard – taking relief from (R26.1)
lifting the ball – adopting incorrect procedure (R12.2)
loose impediments – if the ball moves when moving (R18.2)
lost ball – taking relief for (R27.1)
marking the ball – failing to do so before lifting (R20.1)
out of bounds – taking relief when the ball goes OB (R27.1)
provisional ball – failing to announce intention to play (R27.2)
replacing a ball – moved by wind or rain (R18.1)
tee – using one other than on the teeing ground (R18.2)
water hazard – taking relief from (R26.1)

Types ⑤ stroke and distance

1 stroke penalty plus the requirement that the ball be played
from the place where the previous stroke was played with the
original ball e.g. under the rules relating to **Lost ball** (see **(l10)**)
or **Out of bounds** (see **(o5)**)

Basic rules

Procedure

Basic rules

1 all penalties incurred during a round are cancelled if the round is cancelled – even disqualification (R33.2d)

2 no penalty can be rescinded, modified or imposed after a competition is closed (R34.1b) – except disqualification – see **Disqualification (d7)**

3 a penalty may not be waived by a local rule

Procedure

1 *match play*
(i) if he incurs a penalty the player must inform his opponent as soon as practicable unless he is obviously proceeding under a rule involving a penalty and this has been observed by the opponent
(ii) failure to inform is deemed to be giving **Wrong information** (see **(w8)**) and **loss of hole penalty** applies if the error is not corrected even if the player was not aware that he had incurred the penalty **(a)** (R9.2)

a **application of the penalty**
• *player wins the hole but realises at the next hole that he is playing a wrong ball – an opponent can claim the previous hole even though the player was not aware of the penalty (D9.2/8)*
• *player omits a penalty stroke, his opponent concedes the match and the error is then discovered in the clubhouse – the opponent's claim was valid as the result had not been announced (R2.5) and the player lost the hole and match even though he was not aware of the penalty at the time (D9.2/10)*

Types

2 *stroke play*

(i) the player must inform his marker of the penalty as soon as practicable (R9.3) – but **no penalty** if he doesn't

(ii) **disqualification** penalty can be imposed modified or rescinded after a competition has closed (**b**) (R34.1b) if

– the player has returned a score for any hole lower than that actually taken (unless it was a penalty stroke of which he was not aware)

– the player claimed a higher handicap and this affected the number of strokes received

– it appears that players agreed to waive the rules (**c**)

3 *threesomes/foursomes* – penalty strokes do not affect the order of play (D29.1/5)

(**b**) **competition closed**
• *when results have been officially announced (R34.1b)*

(**c**) **application of penalty**
• *there is no time limit for imposition of the penalty*
– *a player was disqualified for a breach of the rule 3 days after the match had been completed (R34.1a)*
• *but the Committee has discretion to decide timing on the imposition of the penalty in accordance with equity (D34.1b/8) by either*
– *cancelling the competition or*
– *applying the penalty only from the time of discovery or*
– *reinstating the payer last eliminated by the offender or*
– *having all players eliminated by the offender play off*
• *and the Committee can decide to waive the disqualification penalty and substitute a lesser penalty (R33.7)*

p6 PIN

see *Flagstick (f5)*

p7 PITCH MARK (BALL MARK)

see *Ball embedded (b9)* for rules and procedure when a ball is embedded in its own pitch mark

Basic rules

1. through the green – a player is not entitled to relief from a pitch mark **without penalty** unless it was made after his ball came to rest (D13.2/8)

2. on the putting green – ball marks and hole plugs or damage may be repaired but no other damage (a) may be repaired if it might assist the player in his subsequent play of the hole (R16.1c)

a other damage
- player may not tap down spike marks near the hole if they would improve his line of putt (D16.1c/4)
- ball embedded in its own pitch mark on the fairway – player elected to take a drop under R25.2 but before dropping he repaired the pitch mark – **loss of hole/2 stroke penalty** (D13.2/10)
- pitch mark from previous stroke interferes with backswing – the player may not press it down to improve his area of intended swing – **loss of hole/2 stroke penalty** (D13.2/21)

Procedure

if the ball is moved during repair it can be replaced **without penalty**

Penalty

for unauthorised repair – **loss of hole/2 strokes**

Exception

an opponent/fellow competitor may request that a player's ball mark be left as it might assist his play – the player may not then repair it (D16.1c/2)

Royal GC Evian, Switzerland

What is it?

the term for putting the ball back in the exact position (a) from which it was moved when so authorised by the Rules – see also **Dropping the ball (d16)** and **lifting the ball (l4)**

> **a**   **exact position**
> • if the player lifts the ball as allowed by the rules but cannot clean it he may rotate the ball on replacing it so that mud which is stuck to it does not interfere between the club face and the ball (D21.5)

Procedure

1. when required to be placed by the Rules a ball may be placed by the player or his partner (b). If it is being replaced it must be by the player, his partner or the person who moved or lifted it (R20.3a)

2. if the original lie of a ball to be placed or replaced has altered, it should be placed in the nearest similar lie within 1 club length not nearer the hole and not in a hazard (R20.3b) **NB** if the ball is in a hazard it must be placed/replaced as above but in the hazard

3. if a ball or marker is accidentally moved (c) during placing or replacing – it should be replaced **without penalty** (R20.3a)

4. if the ball fails to stay on the spot where it was placed it can be replaced **without penalty**. If it still fails to stay it should be placed on the nearest spot not nearer the hole where it will stay (d) (R20.3d) If it comes to rest on the spot but then moves again – play it as it lies (unless any other Rule applies)

> **b**   **player**
> • in rules relating to placing it is deemed to include a partner (D20.3a/0.5)

5 if it is impossible to determine the spot where the ball is to be placed or replaced it should be dropped (or on the putting green placed) as near as possible to the original spot (R20.3c)

6 a ball placed in a wrong place or dropped when it should have been placed – provided it has not been played may be lifted and replaced **without penalty** (R20.6 and D20.6/1) BUT – a ball placed in wrong place, dropped instead of placed or vice versa and then played (e) – **loss of hole/ 2 stroke penalty** (D20.6/1) (D20.7b/1) – see *Wrong place* (**w9**)

c **accidentally moved**
• ball replaced on the green but the marker was not removed – wind then moved the ball – the ball is in play when replaced even though the marker was not moved – it must be played as it lies in its new position (D20.4/1)
• ball replaced on edge of hole rolls in – if it was at rest for a few seconds before rolling in – deemed to have been holed out with the previous stroke unless it was not replaced on its original spot in which case it must be replaced (D20.3d/1) – see *Ball overhanging the hole* (**b19**)

d **application of the penalty**
• ball placed in wrong place and putted – the player realised his mistake, picked up the ball and played from the correct place – **2 stroke penalty** for playing from a wrong place plus **2 stroke penalty** for lifting without marking and replacing (D20.7b/2)

e **nearest spot**
• ball in rough kept falling vertically when replaced – nearest spot not nearer the hole where it would stay was vertically below its original position – this was the correct spot to place it (D20.3d/3)
• ball in tree knocked down by outside agency – impossible to replace it – must declare it unplayable and proceed accordingly (D18.1/9)
• ball in bunker will not stay on spot and rest of bunker is nearer the hole, so nearest spot is outside bunker. Player must declare ball unplayable and incur penalty (D20.3d/2)

Penalty

1 for failing to place or replace the ball as required by the rules **loss of hole/2 strokes**

2 for replacing a ball when not authorised by the Rules – **1 stroke** (R18.2)

p9 PLUGGED BALL

see *Ball embedded* (b9)

p10 POST

see *Stakes* (s18)

p11 PRACTICE STROKE

What is it?

actually hitting the ball as opposed to a practice swing

Basic rule ❶

Before a round

match play – unless the Committee rules otherwise practice on the course on any day before a round is permitted (R7.1a)

stroke play – unless the Committee rules otherwise practice on the day of the competition on the course or testing the surface of a putting green before a round **is not** permitted (a) and if the competition is over consecutive days (b) or if there is a play off a player may not practice or test the surface of the putting green between rounds

Exceptions to Basic rule ❶

1. practice putting/chipping near the first tee is permitted (R7.1b)

2. a practice swing is permitted at any time

3. **no penalty** if a practice stroke is played in accordance with the exceptions to Rule 7.2 – see Exceptions to Basic rule ❷ p295 – even though there may be a subsequent consecutive round (D7.1b/7)

Penalty

disqualification Ⓒ

Ⓒ application of the penalty
• player played one stroke from the tee into an out of bounds area – Committee would be justified in modifying the penalty to **2 strokes** under R33.7 (D7.1b/1)

ⓐ practice/testing
• caddie practising or testing a green before a round does not subject the player to a penalty as he is only responsible for the caddie during the round (D7.1b/5)

ⓑ consecutive
• 54 hole competition is still deemed consecutive even though the middle round is cancelled (D7.1b/6)

Basic rules ▸

Procedure ▸

Exceptions ▸

Basic rule ②

During a round

practice strokes are not permitted during the play of a hole by a player ⓓ or between the play of 2 holes (R7.2)

ⓓ **play of a hole**
  • is deemed completed in fourball when both partners have holed out (D7.2/1)
• practice putt on the 18th between rounds is only permissible if immediately after holing out (D7.2/8)
• putting on a fairway whilst waiting for the green to clear – **loss of hole/2 stroke penalty** (D7.2/2)
• in a foursome if one partner plays a practice stroke whilst the other tees off this is deemed 'during the play of a hole' – **loss of hole/2 stroke penalty** (D29/3)
• in fourball if A practices putt on previous green whilst B tees from next tee, A incurs **2 stroke penalty** in stroke play and is **disqualified from hole** in match play (D30.3f/12)

Practice strokes in a bunker – even without a club – may be deemed testing its condition – see **(b33)**

What is it?

Basic rule ①

Penalties

Penalty

loss of hole/2 strokes

Exceptions to Basic rule ❷

practice strokes are allowed **without penalty** when:

❶ putting or chipping on or near the putting green of the hole last played ⓔ , the practice putting green or the teeing ground of the next hole to be played in the round

❷ play has been suspended by the Committee – but only as in ❶ above, not on the competition course and as permitted by the Committee **NB** a player cannot practice in a hazard or if the practice would unduly delay play (R7.2)

❸ when playing match play and the strokes are played in continuing the play of a hole which has already been decided (R7.2)

❹ hitting a range ball back to the driving range or ball back to another player – **no penalty** if the intent is only as courtesy or to tidy up the course (D7.2/5 and 5.5)

ⓔ **hole last played**
• even though on a 9 hole course the hole may be played again as part of an 18 hole competition (D7.2/9)

Practice putts are permitted on the tee, but as a matter of etiquette should not be played when another player is teeing off

p12 PRACTICE SWING

What is it?

not actually hitting the ball

Basic rules

1. it is allowed at any time

2. if the ball is accidentally hit – **1 stroke penalty** – see *Ball moved* **(b18)**

3. a practice swing should avoid causing damage to the course, particularly the teeing the ground (EQ)

Vilamoura I GC, Portugal

p13 PREFERRED LIE

What is it?

the practice of being allowed to move the ball a defined length usually 1 club length or up to 6 inches when its lie is affected by adverse weather conditions

Basic rule

this is **not** permitted under the general rules of golf

Procedure

check the local rules before the round – including the distance a player is allowed to move the ball

Penalty

for breach of the local rule
– loss of hole/2 strokes

Exception

it is often permitted under local rules during winter months

p14 PRIORITY ON THE COURSE

Etiquette

in the absence of special rules:

- a single has no priority at all
- a 2 ball has priority over a 3 ball and a 4 ball match
- 3 and 4 ball matches have equal priority
- a match playing a whole round has priority over a match playing a shorter round
- if a match falls more than one hole behind it should invite the players behind to play through (EQ)

p15 PRO-AM

a competition in which a professional and one or more amateurs compete as a team

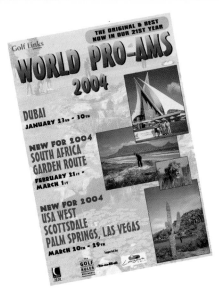

What is it?

a ball played for a ball which may be lost **other than in a water hazard** (a) or may be out of bounds (b) (DF)

– the use of a provisional ball is a procedure to save time as the relief if the original ball turns out to be lost or out of bounds generally requires a player to walk all the way back to the place from which he played his previous stroke to play another ball

– not to be confused with a **Second ball** (see **(s5)**) – which is one played as an alternative when a player is unsure about a rule or procedure affecting the original ball

(a) lost in a water hazard

• provisional played when the original was believed to be in a water hazard – this is not a provisional but a second ball which was then the ball in play (D27.2a/2)

• provisional played when the original was believed to be either lost or in a water hazard – it was then found in the water hazard – provisional to be picked up **without penalty** and the original played under R26 (D27.2c/1) – see **Water hazard (w2)**

(b) lost out of bounds

• provisional played when original believed to be out of bounds – player holed out with the provisional but then found that the original had not been OB – he had therefore played a wrong ball – **loss of hole/2 stroke penalty** plus he had to play original ball from where it lay (D27.2c/3) – see **Wrong ball (w7)**

• provisional played in error in belief that it is the original ball – it becomes the ball in play – **1 stroke penalty** (D27.2b/7)

• provisional lifted when player found his original ball – original ball then seen to be out of bounds – provisional was ball in play and was lifted without authority – **1 stroke penalty** and replace under R18.2a (D27.2b/8) – see **Ball moved (b18)**

Procedure ➜

Procedure

1. the player must announce (a) to his opponent/fellow competitor his intention to play a provisional ball as such before he goes to look for his original ball (D27.2a/1) – if not the provisional automatically becomes the ball in play and a **1 stroke penalty** is incurred

2. the provisional ball must be played from the spot from which the original ball was played – except if played from the teeing ground when it can be played from anywhere within the teeing ground

3. if the provisional ball does not go as far as the original the player may play another stroke or strokes with it until he reaches where he believes the original ball to be and determines whether he can play his original ball or whether he must continue with the provisional ball (R27.2)

4. a provisional ball played from the teeing ground should be played after an opponent/fellow competitor has played his first stroke (R10.3)

(a) **announce**
• *player must specifically refer to a provisional ball- 'I'll play another one' is not sufficient* (D27.20/1)

What is it?

300

5 if the original ball is found within the permitted time – see
Lost ball (l10) – the player must play it and pick up the
provisional (b) (D27.2c/2). The player may not opt to play the
provisional – if he does – **loss of hole/2 stroke penalty** –
see **Wrong ball (w9)**

6 if the original ball is found any penalties incurred in playing
the provisional are cancelled (D15/7) but not penalties
unrelated to the ball itself e.g. giving advice (D15/7)

7 if the provisional ball strikes and moves the original ball –
no penalty – the original ball to be replaced and played
(D18.5/2) – if vice versa – play it as it lies (D19.5/5)

8 a second provisional ball can be utilised if necessary (R27.2a)

(b) **found**
• *player does not have to search
for his original ball – he may opt to
take the appropriate penalty and play
the provisional but an opponent/fellow
competitor can search for the original
ball and if found can require the player
to play it provided player has not
played further stroke at the provisional
ball (D27.2b/1)*
• *player lifted his provisional when he
found his original ball – he played the
original but then discovered it was a
wrong ball – 1 **stroke and distance
penalty** for losing the original ball plus
2 stroke penalty for playing a wrong
ball plus **1 stroke penalty** for picking
up provisional ball (D27.2b/9)*

p17 PUTTER

What is it?

a club designed primarily for use on the putting green (R4.1)

Basic rules

1. **borrowing** – a player may not borrow a fellow competitor's putter to replace his own lost putter – if he does – **2 stroke penalty** (D4.4a/19)

2. **changing** – he may only normally do so during a stipulated round within circumstances permitted under rules relating to number of and damage to clubs – see **Club (c9)**

   for other rules and procedures see **Club (c9)**

Characteristics

see generally under **Club (c9)** but the following amendments apply:

adjustablility – in addition to being adjustable for weight other forms of adjustability are permissible provided that they cannot be readily made, the adjustable parts are firmly fixed and are unlikely to work loose during the round and all configurations conform with the Rules (R4 appendix II 4.1a)

face – putter may have 2 faces but they must be opposite each other and have the same characteristics and loft not exceeding 10 degrees. Specifications relating to club face markings do not apply (R4 appendix II 4.1e)

grip – need not be circular provided there is no concavity and it remains generally similar along the length of the grip. If it has more than one grip, both must be circular and the axis of each must coincide with that of the shaft (R4 appendix II 4.1c)

head – exceptions to plain shape requirements may be acceptable

shaft – may be attached to the head at any point and need not remain in line with the heel

Left: Estoril GC, Portugal

What is it?

the area of the hole being played which is specially prepared for putting or any other area defined as such by the Committee (a) (DF). It does not include the 'fringe' – the area surrounding the putting green which is often cut to a higher level

(a) **defined by the Committee**
• *Committee may publish maps of putting greens showing the position of the holes each day* (D33.6)

Above: Gary Player Country Club, South Africa
Left: Dingle GC, Ireland

Basic rules

Penalty

Etiquette

Basic rules

1 a ball is on the green when any part of it touches the green **(b)** (DF)

2 a ball on the green may be lifted and cleaned **without penalty** at any time unless it is on the wrong green – see **5**

3 ballmarks and hole plugs or damage on the putting green may be repaired; no other damage may be repaired if it might assist a player in his subsequent play of the hole (R16.1c) unless permitted by a local rule

4 a player may not test the surface of the putting green by rolling the ball, or roughening or scraping the green **(c)** (R16.1d)

5 if the ball is on the wrong putting green it must be lifted and dropped **without penalty** at the nearest point of relief being a point within 1 club length of the point on the course but off the green nearest to the original spot but not nearer the hole, not in a hazard and not on a putting green **(d)** (R25.3). The player must not play the ball from the wrong green. Any strokes played on the wrong green count towards the score – in addition to the penalty (D25.3/2)

d **putting green**
• *putting green includes practice putting and chipping greens*
• *includes a double green unless specifically divided off by stakes (D25.3/1) or a line*

What is it?

306

b touches

• ball on the putting green sitting on mud attached
to it is deemed on the green *(D16/1)*
• ball is off the green but a lump of mud on the side of the
ball overhangs and touches the green – the ball is
deemed off the green *(D16/1)*

c testing

• caddie roughens surface of the green but does not give any
information to player – **loss of hole/2 strokes penalty** *(D16.1d/6)*
• caddie practising or testing a green before a round – **no penalty**
as the player is only responsible for the caddie during round
(D7.1b/5)
• casual action e.g. rolling ball back to a player or to its mark is not
deemed testing *(D16.1d/1 and 3)* – unless an intent to test can be
implied *(D16.1d/2)*
• placing hand on the green to determine wetness –
no penalty *(D16.1d/4)*
• rubbing ball on the green to clean it – not deemed testing *(D16.1d/5)*
• in a 36 hole competition on consecutive days a player may not test
the surface between rounds *(D7.1b/5.5)*

Penalty

for breach of rules – **loss of hole/2 strokes**

Etiquette

1 damage made by the ball should be carefully repaired

2 spike damage can only be repaired on completion of the hole

3 no damage should be done by leaning on the putter, putting
down golf bags or flagstick or by standing close to the hole

307

r1 RAKE

see *Bunker* **(b33)** and *Obstructions – moveable* **(o3)**

Procedure

rakes should be placed outside bunkers as far away as is practical
and where they are least likely to interfere with play (D misc/2)

r2 RED

- **red lines/stakes** – delineate the boundaries of *Lateral water
hazards* (see **(l1)**)

- **red tee markers** – indicate the ladies teeing area

Above: Emirates GC, Dubai
Left: Plantation GC, Amelia Island, Florida

r3 | REFEREE

What is it?

a person appointed by the Committee (a) to accompany players
and decide questions of fact and apply the Rules (DF)

> **(a) appointed by the Committee**
> • a person not so appointed gives a wrong
> ruling in match play – ruling stands (D2.5/8)

Procedure

1 he has authority to act on a breach of the Rules seen by or
reported to him

2 he cannot attend the flagstick, stand at or mark the position
of the hole, lift or mark the position of the ball

3 he may warn a player about to infringe a Rule – but is under
no duty to do so (R34.2/3)

4 if appointed by the Committee his decision is final **(b)** (R34.2)

> **(b) final**
> • even though it may be wrong –
> referee authorised a player to infringe
> a rule – **no penalty** because decision
> was by definition correct (D34.2/2)
> • once a player plays his next stroke a
> referee cannot subsequently change
> his decision (D34.2/5)

r4 REPLACING THE BALL

see *Placing/replacing the ball (p8)*

r5 REPLAYING A STROKE

see *Stroke (s26)*

r6 ROUGH

What is it?

not a term used in the rules of golf. It is the general name commonly applied to all areas of the course other than the tees, greens, bunkers and water and which are not closely mown as fairways

Procedure

because the rules do not differentiate between fairways and rough (other than when a ball is embedded in its own pitch mark – see *Ball embedded (b9)*) – it is sometimes possible to drop out of the rough on to a fairway when taking relief which is permitted under the rules e.g. if ground under repair is just in the rough and one club length from the permitted point of relief includes fairway it is permissible to drop in the fairway even though the ball was originally in the rough

r7 ROUND

see *Stipulated round* (**s23**)

r8 RUB OF THE GREEN

the term used when a moving ball is accidentally stopped or
deflected by an outside agency and no relief is permitted (DF)
– see *Ball deflected* (**b8**)

r9 RULES

What is it?

the Rules of Golf as published by the R&A/USGA and include local rules made by the Committee (DF) conditions of the competition and Decisions on the Rules of Golf

Basic rule

1. failure to comply with a Rule which affects the rights of other players will result in **disqualification** (R3.4)

2. a player is responsible for knowing the Rules (R6.1)

3. a player knowingly giving wrong information on the rules may be **disqualified** (D9/1)

4. the Rules may not be modified by local rules other than as approved by the R&A/USGA (R33.8)

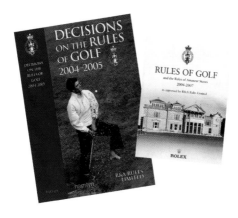

Left: Hyatt Dorado, Puerto Rico

313

The rules

the chronological listing of the rules and their principal corresponding references in this dictionary are as follows:

Rule 1 – *agreement* (**a6**); *golf*; *influencing the movement of the ball* (**i9**); *equity* (**e6**)

Rule 2 – *claim* (**c7**); *concede* (**c15**); *half* (**h1**); *match play* (**m3**)

Rule 3 – *hole out* (**h7**); *rules*; *second ball* (**s3**)

Rule 4 – *club* (**c9**); *putter* (**p17**)

Rule 5 – *ball – characteristics* (**b5**); *ball unfit for play* (**b22**)

Rule 6 – *delay* (**d3**); *discontinuance* (**d6**); *handicap* (**h2**); *identifying the ball*; *rules of a competition*; *scorecard* (**s3**); *suspension of play* (**d6**); *tee time* (**t3**)

Rule 7 – *practice* (**p11**)

Rule 8 – *advice* (**a4**); *line of play/putt* (**l7**)

Rule 9 – *penalty* (**p5**); *wrong information* (**w8**)

Rule 10 – *order of play* (**o4**)

Rule 11 – *addressing the ball* (**a2**); *teeing ground* (**t4**); *tee markers* (**t2**)

Rule 12 – *identifying the ball* (**i2**); *searching for the ball* (**s4**)

Rule 13 – *area of intended swing* (**a14**); *bunker* (**b33**); *hazard*; *lateral water hazard* (**l1**); *lie of the ball* (**l3**); *line of play/putt* (**l7**); *water hazard* (**w2**)

Rule 14 – *artificial devices* (**a12**); *assistance* (**a13**); *ball struck more than once* (**b21**); *moving ball* (**b8**); *stroke* (**s26**)

Rule 15 – *exchanging balls* (**e8**); *substituting a ball* (**s31**); *wrong ball* (**w7**)

Rule 16 – *ball overhanging hole* (**b19**); *hole* (**h6**); *lifting the ball* (**l4**); *line of play/putt* (**l7**); *putting green* (**p18**)

Rule 17 – *attending the flagstick* (**a14**); *flagstick* (**f5**)

What is it?

Basic rule

r10 RULES OF A COMPETITION

a player is responsible for knowing the rules under which a competition is to be played (R6.1)

S1 · SAFETY

a player should always make sure that he is unlikely to hit anyone with his club, ball or any debris which might be moved by his swing or stroke (EQ)

S2 · SAND TRAP

see *Bunker* (b33)

S3 · SCORECARD

Basic rules

1. the player is responsible for the correctness of his score at each hole (R6.6d)

2. he is not responsible for the addition of the card or the application of his recorded handicap – this is the responsibility of the Committee (a) (R33.5)

a responsibility of the Committee

• as addition is the responsibility of the Committee – **no penalty** against a player for incorrect addition *(D6.6d/2)*

• *player recorded the correct scores but the Committee added them up wrongly – the player would have won the competition but the Committee ordered a play off between two others in second place – the addition error was discovered before the result was announced – the player must be reinstated as the winner (D34.1b/5)*

• *if discovered after results announced the Committee must rectify the error (D34.1b/6)*

• *if a player plays off the wrong handicap as posted on a notice board by the Committee this is the Committee's error and must be rectified by them – if as a result the player has recorded a lower score than that taken –* **1 stroke** *must be added to his score as the player had played off 17 handicap when his actual handicap was 16 (D6.2b/3)*

• *but if the Committee puts the wrong handicap on his scorecard and the player does not correct it – this is his responsibility and he will be* **disqualified** *(D6.2b/3.5)*

Penalty

if he has recorded a lower score than that taken –
disqualified (b)

if higher – the higher score counts *(R6.6d)*

b application of the penalty

• *a player will* **not be disqualified** *if he records a lower score because he has not included a penalty of which he was not aware before the competition closed (R34.1b (iii))*

• *nor if he records a lower score than that taken if it does not affect his overall score e.g. in Stableford if he records a 7 instead of 8 he still gets 0 points (D32.2a/4)*

Left: Cabo del Sol GC, Mexico

Procedure →

Penalty →

Alterations →

Procedure

1 prior to the commencement of the round the player should arrange for a fellow competitor to mark his card and should hand his card to that person

2 it is advisable for the player to also keep his own record of his own score

3 the player should check his card after completion of the round, ensuring the correct gross scores are recorded against the appropriate holes (**a**). Any doubtful points should be settled with the Committee

4 in stroke play he must ensure his handicap is recorded on the card

5 he must ensure the marker (**b**) has signed the card

6 he must sign the card himself (**c**) except in match play

7 he must return the card to the Committee as soon as possible (R6.6b) but the Committee cannot require him to enter his score into a computer (D6.6a/8)

8 if the original card is lost a duplicate may be prepared and returned (D6.6a/7)

9 In competitions, the Committee must provide each player with a scorecard containing the date and his name

Basic rules

Penalty

a correct score

- omission of score for one hole but total still correct – **disqualified** (D6.6d/1)
- error made in recording scores for first 9 holes in boxes for 10-18 and vice versa – **disqualified** for recording against some holes scores lower than actually taken (D6.6d/3)
- error made by A recording B's scores on A's own card and vice versa (i.e. cards not exchanged) – **disqualified** for recording against some holes scores lower than actually taken (D6.6d/4)
- score recorded by a player and marker were challenged by spectators – Committee may take into account spectators testimony – if accepted player **disqualified** (D6.6d/5)
- knowingly wrongly attested by marker – marker **disqualified** (D1.3/6)

b marker

- one or more markers must attest the entire round – a card will not be accepted if a marker was not present for say 3 or 4 holes (D6.6a/2)

c sign

- signatures need not be in the correct places – **no penalty** (D6.6b/1)
- initials instead of signature – **no penalty** (D6.6b/2)
- in 36 hole competition signature omitted from first round card but correct on second round card – **disqualified** (D6.6b/3)
- unsigned card not noticed by Committee – result announced and omission subsequently noticed – **no penalty** and result stands unless the player knew of his omission before the competition closed (D34.1b/2)

d returned

- means delivered to the committee AND the player has left the designated 'scoring area' (D6.6c/1) but this does not apply if the card has to be posted into a box

Penalty

for breach of any of ④ – ⑧ opposite – **disqualification**

Alterations

see **Stableford**
competition (s16)

see Basic Rule ❷ see Procedure ❷

see Procedure ❸

see Procedure ❹

see Procedure ❶

see Alterations
❶ and ❷

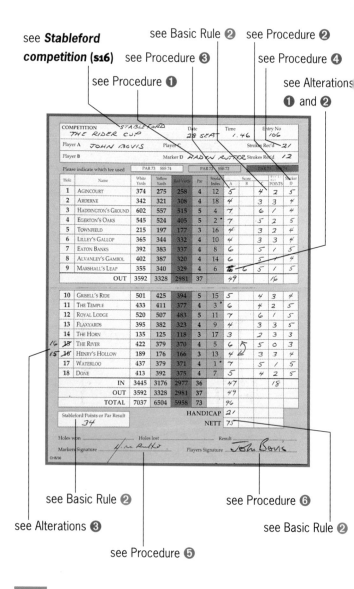

COMPETITION	STABLEFORD			Date		Time		Entry No	
THE RIDER CUP				28 SEPT		1.46		106	

Player A	JOHN BOVIS	Player C			Strokes Rec'd	21
Player B		Marker D	HADYN RUTTER		Strokes Rec'd	12

Please indicate which tee used   PAR 73 SSS 74   PAR 72 SSS 72   PAR 73 SSS 74

Hole	Name	White Yards	Yellow Yards	Red Yards	Par	Stroke Index	Score A	Score B	Par or Net POINTS	Marker D
1	AGINCOURT	374	275	258	4	12	5		4	2	5
2	ARDERNE	342	321	308	4	18	4		3	3	4
3	HADDINGTON'S GROUND	602	557	515	5	4	7		6	1	4
4	EGERTON'S OAKS	545	524	405	5	2 *	7		5	2	5
5	TOWNFIELD	215	197	177	3	16	4		3	2	4
6	LILLEY'S GALLOP	365	344	332	4	10	4		3	3	4
7	EATON BANKS	392	383	337	4	8	6		5	1	5
8	ALVANLEY'S GAMBOL	402	387	320	4	14	6		5	1	4
9	MARSHALL'S LEAP	355	340	329	4	6	5̶ 6		5	1	5
	OUT	3592	3328	2981	37		49		16	

10	GRISELL'S RIDE	501	425	394	5	15	5		4	3	4
11	THE TEMPLE	433	411	377	4	3 *	6		4	2	5
12	ROYAL LODGE	520	507	483	5	11	7		6	1	5
13	FLAXYARDS	395	382	323	4	9	4		3	3	5
14	THE HORN	135	125	118	3	17	3		2	3	3
16 15	THE RIVER	422	379	370	4	5	6	5	5	0	3
15 16	HENRY'S HOLLOW	189	176	166	3	13	4	2	3	3	4
17	WATERLOO	437	379	371	4	1 *	7		5	1	5
18	DONE	413	392	375	4	7	5		4	2	5
	IN	3445	3176	2977	36		47		18	
	OUT	3592	3328	2981	37		49			
	TOTAL	7037	6504	5958	73		96			

Stableford Points or Par Result	HANDICAP	21
34	NETT	75

Holes won	Holes lost	Result
Markers Signature	H. Rutter	Players Signature John Bovis

CH8/96

see Basic Rule ❷

see Procedure ❻

see Alterations ❸

see Basic Rule ❷

see Procedure ❺

Alterations

1. cannot be made after the card has been returned to the Committee (R6.6c)

2. need not be initialled and the Committee cannot require them to be initialled (D6.6a/6)

3. if the scores are entered in the right sequence but against the wrong hole numbers – the marker can alter hole numbers on the card to ensure an accurate record (D6.6a/3)

4. made after the marker has signed the card and left the course – the player should consult the Committee before altering – if not, **disqualification** – (D6.6b/7)

S4   SEARCHING FOR THE BALL

What is it?

time allowed – 5 minutes, after which Lost ball rules and procedure apply – see **Lost ball (L10)** for interpretation of 5 minute rule

Preliminary

The rules vary according to whether the player is searching:

(i)	through the green	(page 324)
(ii)	in a hazard/bunker	(page 325)
(iii)	in a water hazard	(page 326)

(i) through the green

Basic rules

1. the player must not move the ball or cause it to be moved during the search – if he does – **1 stroke penalty** (R18.2)

2. he may touch or bend long grasses, rushes, bushes etc. but only to the extent necessary to find and identify the ball and provided this does not improve the lie, area of intended swing or line of play (R12.1)

3. if an opponent or fellow competitor moves the ball during the search – **no penalty** (R18.3 and 4) and replace the ball

4. see also *Identifying the ball* **(i2)**

Exception

in casual water, ground under repair, a hole, cast or runway made by a burrowing animal, reptile or bird, a lateral water hazard or a water hazard – **no penalty** if the ball is accidentally moved; the ball must be replaced unless the player elects to take relief under the relevant relief provisions (R12.1)

What is it?

Preliminary

(ii) in a hazard/bunker

Basic rule

1 if the ball is covered (a) by **Loose impediments** (see **(l9)**) or sand a player may remove them by probing, raking or other means (b) but only enough to see a part of the ball sufficient to identify it (R12.1) even if it means touching the sand in a bunker (D12.1/4)

2 **no penalty** if the ball is accidentally moved in a water hazard or lateral water hazard – ball to be replaced unless the player opts to take relief under the relevant provisions

3 for rules and procedures in a bunker – see **Bunker (b33)**

(a) **covered**
• it is sufficient if the ball is visible and identifiable from any angle – it need not be visible from the address position (D12.1/3)

(b) **other means**
• e.g. using the clubhead (D12.1/1)

Procedure

if excess material is removed and/or the ball is moved – the ball must be covered up again and replaced so that only part is visible – **no penalty** (R12.1)

Penalty

for breaches of R12.1 – **loss of hole/2 strokes**

325

(iii) in a water hazard

Basic rule

the player may probe with a club or otherwise but if the ball is kicked during the search –**1 stroke penalty & replace it** (D12.1/5)

Procedure

if the ball is moved it must be replaced **without penalty** unless the player elects to take relief under R26.1 – see **Water hazard (w2)**

S5 SECOND BALL

What is it?

one played as an alternative when a player is in doubt about a rule or procedure affecting the original ball. Not to be confused with a **Provisional ball** (see **(p16)**) – which is one played to save time when the original ball may be lost or out of bounds

Basic rules

in stroke play

1 where the player is in doubt as to a rule or procedure he may **without penalty** play a second ball (a) (R3.3) in accordance with the procedures outlined on page 328

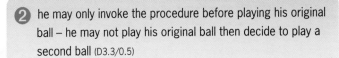

❷ he may only invoke the procedure before playing his original ball – he may not play his original ball then decide to play a second ball (D3.3/0.5)

in match play these procedures are **not** available and a second ball is therefore a **Wrong ball** (see **(w7)**) and hole will be lost if properly claimed by an opponent (D3.3/9)

a   second ball

• second ball is not a provisional ball but a provisional ball may be a second ball (D3.3/1)
• second ball played despite ruling by Committee member (duly authorised) that the player was not entitled to relief – score with the original ball must count plus **2 stroke penalty** for undue delay (D3.3/2)
• player plays from tee in wrong order – abandons first ball and plays second ball in correct order – original ball became a lost ball and the second ball became the ball in play – **1 stroke penalty** under lost ball rules (D10.2c/1)
• rule invoked only after having played out of problem situation and then realising relief might have been available – original ball counts (**no penalty**) (D3.3/6)
• second second ball – cannot be played (D3.3/10)
• strikes original ball (both on putting green) – **2 shot penalty** if the second ball is the scoring ball – **no penalty** if the original ball is the scoring ball (D3.3/7)
• player did not adopt second ball procedure but dropped original in a position which complied both with ball unplayable rules and ground under repair rules as he thought the the area was GUR even though it was not marked as such – after the round he sought a ruling from the Committee before submitting his scorecard – it was not GUR so he **added a penalty stroke** to his score (D3.3/11)

Procedure ➤

Penalty ➤

Procedure

1. the player must first inform his marker or fellow competitor of his intent to invoke the Rule (R3.3a)

2. he must nominate before playing his first ball the ball he wishes to count for his score if both balls turn out to have been played in accordance with the Rules (b)

3. he should report the facts to the Committee for a ruling before returning his score card

4. if a second ball is played, subsequent strokes and penalty strokes incurred with the ball which is not used for the score do not count - unless they would apply whichever ball was used e.g. on giving advice (D20.7b/6) or for playing a wrong ball (D15/7)

5. having declared his intention to play a second ball the player may only change his mind before taking further action e.g. putting the second ball and play or playing his original ball (D3.3/7.5)

Penalty

if he fails to do 1 or 2 above the score with the original ball counts in any event – **disqualification** if procedure 3 is not followed – (R3.3)

What is it?

Basic rules

b   **the ball he wishes to count**
  • *if no selection made the original ball counts if deemed played in accordance with the Rules (D3.3/0.5)*
• *if neither ball is played in accordance with the Rules:*
  – where the ball was played from a wrong place and there was no other serious breach with either ball – the original ball score counts plus an additional penalty under the applicable Rule (D3.3/0.5)
  – as above but serious breach with one ball – the other ball score counts plus the penalty as above (D3.3/0.5)
  – as above but serious breach with both balls –
  disqualified *(D3.3/0.5)*

 # SIDE

one or more players who are partners (DF)

SINGLE

a match when one person plays against another (DF)

SINGLE PLAYER

• has no priority on the course (EQ)

• in match play if a single player who is not part of the match is invited to join for the round by one player the opponent can object and if the single still plays the opponent can claim the match (D2/1)

S9 SIXES

matchplay game for 4 players playing as 2 sides. Each player plays 6 holes as partner with each of the other 3 players. For each 6 holes the winners receive 2 points each or all 4 receive one point each if the match is halved. The overall winner is the individual with most points

S10 SKINS

game in which scoring is by holes won. If a hole is not won outright by one player then the next hole counts as two for the winner. Similarly if there is no result on the second hole the third hole counts as three for the winner

S11 SLOW PLAY

see *Delay* (**d3**)

S12 SNOW

can be *Casual water* (see (**c4**)) or a *Loose impediment* (see (**l9**)) at the option of the player

S13 SPIKE MARKS

on the putting green

Basic rules

1 may not be tapped down as this is deemed improving the
Line of putt (see **(l17)**) – **loss of hole/2 stroke penalty**

2 an agreement to repair
spike marks is an
Agreement (see **(a6)**)
to waive rules –
disqualification (D1.3/3)

Exception

repairing spike marks after
completion of the hole as a
courtesy to players who
subsequently play the hole is
permitted **without penalty**

S14 SPIKES

are not subject to the rules

S15 SPRINKLER HEADS

see **Obstruction – immoveable (o3)**

What is it?

a game when scoring is by points for each hole (R32.1b)

Procedure

1 after deducting the relevant handicap allowance from the gross score at each hole the points scored are:

hole played in more than one over par	0 points
no return on a hole	0 points
one stroke over par	1 point
par	2 points
one stroke under par	3 points
two under par	4 points
three under par	5 points
four under par	6 points

2 variations

	Denver	Murphy
hole played in more than one over par	– 3 points	– 1 point
one stroke over par	– 1 point	– 1 point
par	0 points	0 points
one stroke under par	2 points	2 points
two under par	5 points	4 points
three under par	8 points	4 points

3 the marker is only responsible for recording the gross number of strokes at each hole; the Committee is responsible for applying the handicap and recording the points total

4 the honour is determined by the best net score at the previous hole (D32.1/3)

5 if a player omits one or more holes he may still return a valid score card – he is deemed to have scored no points on the omitted holes (D32.1/2)

Penalties

1 a competitor is **disqualified from the competition** for breaches of the Rules relating to (R32.2a):

agreements to waive rules

refusal to comply with rules

illegal ball

repeated undue delay

handicap breaches

time for starting

more than one caddie

score card irregularities (a)

non conforming clubs

use of devices/unusual equipment

discontinuance of play

practice before/between rounds

2 when other rules breaches require disqualification it is interpreted as relating to **disqualification from the hole** where the breach took place (R32.2b)

3 for breach of the 14 club rule – **deduct 2 points for each hole** at which breach occurred with **maximum penalty of 4 points**

a **irregularities**
• if the irregularity does not affect the correct team score in a team competition the offender **will not be disqualified** (D32.2a/1)

S17 STAKED TREE

see **Tree (t14)**

S18 STAKES

- **red stakes** – denote a lateral **Water hazard** (see **(w2)**)
- **yellow stakes** – denote a **Water hazard** (see **(w2)**) other than a lateral water hazard
- **white stakes** – denote **Out of bounds** (see **(o5)**)
- **green top** – denote environmentally sensitive areas **(e4)**

stakes are obstructions for rules purposes
– see **Obstructions (o3)** for relevant rules and procedures

S19 STANCE

What is it?

taking his stance consists of a player placing his feet in position for and preparatory to making a stroke (DF)

for rules and procedure relating to interference with stance by **Casual water** (see **(c4)**), **Ground under repair** (see **(g9)**) and holes/casts or runways made by **Burrowing animals** (see **(b34)**) see the relevant entries – see also **Area of intended swing (a11)**)

Basic rule

1. a player may place his feet firmly when taking his stance – but he is not permitted to 'build' a stance ⓐ – (R13.3)

2. he may not improve his **area of stance** – see **a11**

Penalty

loss of hole/2 strokes

Exception

if the player can correct his error in building a stance before he plays and he does so – **no penalty** – e.g. if he was standing on his golf cart and he gets off before playing the stroke
NB – if he has moved sand or earth etc it is impossible for him to restore it to its exact original position so he will be penalised in any event (D13.3/5)

Standing on a cart or kneeling on a towel are not permitted

a **building a stance**
 • *kneeling on towel to prevent trousers getting wet when playing a stroke is deemed building a stance (D13.3/2)*
• *knocking down sand from the side of a bunker to make a level stance (D13.3/3) –* **loss of hole/2 stroke penalty**
• *using a mat to stand on on the teeing ground (D13.3/1) –* **loss of hole/2 stroke penalty**
• *in a bunker 'digging in' to create a firm stance is acceptable BUT see also* **Bunker (b33)** *– for possible problems – deemed to be testing the condition of the sand*

335

S20 STANDARD SCRATCH SCORE

What is it?

- the total score which a scratch player (one having a 0 handicap) would be expected to make in ideal conditions over an 18 hole golf course depending on the yardage measured from the medal tees and the difficulty of the terrain (CNGU)

- unlike par it is not allocated against individual holes but given as a total for the course

up to 4200 yards / 3840 metres SSS 60			5950	5441	68
4400	4023	61	6200	5669	69
4600	4206	62	6400	5852	70
4800	4389	63	6600	6035	71
5000	4572	64	6800	6218	72
5200	4755	65	7000	6401	73
5450	4983	66	7200	6584	74
5700	5212	67			

S21 STATIONARY BALL MOVED

see *Ball moved* (b18) for relevant rules and procedure

S22 STIMP

a means of measuring the relative speed of the greens on different courses

What is it?

playing the holes of the course (18 unless fewer are authorised
by the Committee) in their correct sequence as authorised by the
Committee (a) (DF)

(a) **correct sequence**
  • *teeing off at 9th before holing out at 8th (to avoid long walk)
  is not a stipulated round – **disqualified** (D1.1/1)*
• *playing 2 holes that were excluded from the competition even
  though not counting their scores is not a stipulated round (D3.2/)*

Penalty

for playing in the wrong sequence – **loss of hole/2 strokes**
NB in stroke play, if the error is not corrected before playing from
the next treeing ground – **disqualification** (R11.4b)

for rules when a hole is played out of sequence see ***Teeing
ground* (t4)**

S24 **STONES**

see ***Loose impediments* (l9)**

a game in which each player is given a piece of string which is 1 metre long for each stroke of his handicap (a 13 handicap player gets a 13m string). During the round he may move his ball for any purpose but when he does so he must cut from the string a piece equivalent to the distance he has moved his ball. Once he has used up the length of his string he receives no further concessions. No handicap allowance and the player who completes the round in fewest strokes wins

S26 STROKE

What is it?

the forward movement of the club **a** made with the intention **b** of fairly striking at and moving the ball **c**
NB if the downswing is checked voluntarily before impact this is not deemed a stroke **d** (DF)

see also **Practice stroke (p11)**

a club
  • only one club may be used for a stroke – player held two clubs together for greater impact in long grass – **loss of hole/2 stroke penalty** (D14.1/7)
  • club head comes off at top of backswing but the player still completes the stroke – does not count because the shaft by itself is not a club (D14.2)
  • back of club head may be used for a stroke (D14.1/1)

b intention
  • swing made instinctively in anger as opposed to deliberately is not a stroke provided the player does not hit the ball (D14/6)

C   at the ball

   • swing made at a tree in which
the ball is lodged is not a stroke as it
was not made at the ball *(D14/7)*
• ball resting against boundary fence –
player hit the other side of the fence to
move the ball – deemed a fair stroke –
no penalty *(D14.1/5)*

d   checking the downswing

   • if club head comes off during downswing and the player
continues with his stroke this counts as a stroke – because there
has been a forward movement with the complete
club *(D14/3)* – but it does not count if he stops his stroke
• club broke during downswing – player continued stroke but missed
the ball – separated clubhead hit the ball and moved it – stroke
counts and the ball must be played where it lies *(D14/5)*
• downswing impeded/deflected by outside agency e.g. branch – still
deemed to have made a stroke *(D14/1)*
• downswing altered to deliberately miss the ball is deemed to have
been checked voluntarily *(D14/1.5)*

*Only one club may be
used for a stroke*

Basic rules

Procedure

Penalty

Basic rules

1 the ball must be hit with club head and not pushed scraped or spooned (a) (R14.1)

2 a player must not accept physical assistance from anyone or protection from the elements (b) whilst making a stroke (R14.2)

3 the ball may be struck only once by the club in course of a stroke (c) – **penalty** for multiple strike – **1 stroke** (R14.4) – see *Ball struck more than once* **(b21)**

4 on the putting green a player may not make a stroke whilst another ball on the green is still in motion from a stroke played on the green **except – no penalty** if it is the player's turn to play (R16.1f)

5 when under the Rules a player elects to replay a stroke from where his previous stroke was played, if it was from:
the teeing ground – it can be replayed from anywhere on the teeing ground
through the green or from a hazard – the ball must be dropped and on the putting green the ball must be placed (R20.5)

Procedure

other players should not talk, stand close or move behind the ball when a player is making a stroke (EQ)

Penalty

unless otherwise specified –
loss of hole/2 stroke

What is it?

a club head

- *using putter with billiard type stroke is deemed pushing – **loss of hole/2 stroke penalty*** (D14.1/2)
- *putt with putter handle – **loss of hole/2 stroke penalty*** (D14.1/3)
- *holding club against the ball with one hand and striking the shaft with the other hand to move the ball is deemed pushing – **loss of hole/2 stroke penalty*** (D14.1/6)

b physical assistance/protection from the elements (see **(a13)**)

- *player aligned his partner's putter but stepped away before the partner played the stroke – **no penalty** because prohibition of assistance does not apply prior to making stroke* (D14.2/1)
- *player held his own umbrella in one hand whilst making a stroke with the other – **no penalty** because prohibition only applies if protection is given by someone else* (D14.2/2)
- *caddie may not shield a player from the sun whilst he makes a stroke* (D14.2/3)

c in the course of a stroke

- *ball struck straight up in the air and landed on mud on club face – not an illegal stroke but a breach of **R19.2 (ball deflected by player) – loss of hole/2 stroke penalty** plus drop the ball as near as possible to where it stuck to club* (D14.4/1)
  NB** (D1.4/2) – allowed a ball played from sand and stuck to club in similar circumstances to be dropped **without penalty
- *ball rebounding off pipeline struck club – **no penalty*** (D14.4/2)

S27 STROKE AND DISTANCE

the general term for the penalty which requires the player to incur a penalty stroke and also to return to the point from which the previous stroke was played in order to play his next stroke e.g. when proceeding under the rules relating to a lost ball

S28 STROKE INDEX

the order of difficulty of the holes on a golf course as indicated on the score card for the course. It is used to determine the holes at which players receive their handicap allowance. Thus a 5 handicap player is entitled to deduct 1 stroke from his gross score at each of the 5 most difficult holes – those numbered stroke index 1–5

S29 STROKE PLAY

What is it?

the form of competition where the winner is the one who plays the stipulated round(s) in the fewest strokes (R3.1)

Basic rule

stroke play and match play competitions cannot be played simultaneously – if they are, results should be disregarded by the Committee (R33.1)

342

S30 STROKES

Basic rules

in *match play* – an opponent is entitled to ascertain the number of strokes taken during the play of that hole and also after the hole is completed (a) (R9.2)

in *stroke play* – there is no such entitlement but a player should inform his marker as soon as possible if he incurs a penalty stroke (R9.3)

> ### a play of hole/after hole is completed
> • if a player asks his opponent during the play of a hole how many strokes he has taken – the opponent can reply at any time before the player plays his next stroke (D9.2/4)

S31 SUBSTITUTING A BALL

What is it?

a ball put in play in replacement of the original ball if it is lost, out of bounds, lifted or unfit for play

Basic rule

a ball may not be substituted other than as permitted by the Rules – usually only if it is lost (see **Lost ball (l9)**) or damaged (see **Ball unfit for play (b22)**) or has been moved and cannot easily be recovered (see **Ball moved b18**) or between the play of holes (a) – if it is wrongly substituted it becomes the ball in play (R15.1) and if played the **penalty** is incurred

Penalty

Exception

343

S31 | Substituting a ball

a **example**
• ball thrown to caddie who missed it and ball was lost in a lake – player substituted new ball and putted out – **loss of hole/2 stroke penalty** (D15.2/1) also for ball deliberately thrown into lake in anger (D18.2a/13.5)
• player marked and lifted his ball on the green but then accidentally replaced it with another ball – **loss of hole/2 stroke penalty**

Penalty

loss of hole/2 stroke

Exception

if the error is discovered and corrected before a stroke is played with the substituted ball there is **no penalty** **b**

b **discovered and corrected**
• ball marked on green but inadvertently replaced with a different ball – error discovered and corrected before stroke played – **no penalty** (D15.1/7)
• ball on cart path lifted under R24.2b (see **Obstructions (o3)**) but a different ball was mistakenly dropped under the relief procedure – error discovered before next stroke – must lift and drop the original ball – **no penalty** (D20.6/3)

Basic rule

S32 | SUSPENSION OF PLAY

see **Discontinuance (d6)**

S33 | SWING

see **Area of intended swing (a11)** and **Practice swing (p12)**

What is it?

the means used to raise the ball off the ground for the purpose of
a stroke from the teeing ground It must not be longer than 4
inches (101.6mm)

Basic rules

1 for the purpose of a stroke from the teeing ground the ball
may be placed on the ground, on an irregularity of surface
created by the player on the ground, or on a tee, sand or
other substance to raise it off the ground (R11.1)

2 if a ball not in play falls off the tee or is knocked off it by the
player in addressing it, it may be re teed **without penalty**
(a) (R11.3) – see **Addressing the ball (a2)**

3 a tee may not be used for the purpose of a stroke from any
other part of the course – if it is **1 stroke penalty**
– see **Ball moved (b18)**

a **re teed**
• *ball missed completely from tee shot – player lowers the
tee before playing again – he is deemed to have moved the ball
and not replaced it – **penalty – loss of hole/1 stroke** for
moving the ball **plus 1 stroke** for not replacing it (D18.2a/1)*
• *ball nudged off tee from tee shot – player puts it back on the tee
before playing again – he is deemed to have moved the ball and
not replaced it **loss of hole/1 stroke penalty** for moving the
ball **plus 1 stroke** for not replacing it (D18.2a/2)*

Penalty

for use of non conforming tee - **disqualification**

t2 | TEE MARKER

What is it?

the markers which delineate the front and sides of the teeing ground

Colours

recommended colour codes:

blue	championship tees
white	mens medal tees
yellow	mens forward medal tees/visitors' tees
red	ladies medal tees

Basic rule

1. when playing the first stroke from the teeing ground tee markers are deemed to be fixed – a player may not move them or allow them to be moved in order to avoid interference with his stance, area of intended swing or line of play – **if moved loss of hole/2 stroke penalty** (R11.2); if deliberately relocated – **disqualified** (D11.2/2) if accidentally moved or kicked and relocated prior to playing - **no penalty** (D11.2/2)

2. at all other times they are deemed to be **Obstructions** (see **(o3)**) (D11.2/1)

Procedure

if they are missing – play should be discontinued until the Committee resolves the problem; but if players estimate their location and no advantage is gained the Committee may accept scores **without penalty** (D11.4b/2)

347

t3 | TEE TIME

What is it?

referred to in the Rules as time of starting (R6.3a)

Exception

the Committee may provide in the rules of a competition that if a player arrives at the teeing ground ready to play but up to 5 minutes late the **penalty may be loss of first hole/2 strokes** instead of **disqualification** (R6.3b)

Dubai Creek GC

Basic rule

if a player is late for his tee time as specified by the Committee
the **penalty is disqualification** (a)

(a) **late**

• third member of group arrived 2 minutes late but still in time
to play in the correct order – **disqualified** because all members of a
group must be present at the allocated start time unless the 5 minute
rule is invoked by the Committee *(D6.3a/2)*
• getting lost, heavy traffic, car breaking down do not justify waiving
the disqualification penalty but being in an accident may *(D6.3a/3)*
• in match play if both are late even though one arrives before the
other the hole is deemed halved *(D6.3a/3)*
• if it is impossible to start at the appointed time (e.g. bad weather)
there is no penalty if one player arrives late *(D6.3a/4)*

What is it?

the starting place for the hole to be played. Rectangular in shape and 2 clubs (any club) length deep. The front and sides are the outside limits of the two tee markers (DF)
– see also **Tee marker (t2)**

Basic rules

1 it is a player's responsibility to know the correct sequence of holes and the teeing ground from which to play (a)

2 a player may stand outside the teeing ground to play a ball within it (R11.1)

3 a ball is outside the teeing ground only when all of it lies outside

4 a ball played from outside the teeing ground is not in play – so any additional penalties or procedures e.g. if it goes out of bounds, do not apply (D11.4b/6)

a **players responsibility**
• *players who played from the wrong teeing ground because the Committee had not indicated hole numbers on the teeing ground – **disqualified** because it was their responsibility for knowing the stipulated round (D11.5/2)*

b **replay**
• *ball played out of bounds from the wrong teeing ground, opponent did not ask for the stroke to be replayed – the original ball is deemed in play and a second ball must be dropped (not teed) on the wrong teeing ground (D11.5/3)*

Procedure

1 when a ball is played from outside the teeing ground or from the wrong teeing ground:

– in *match play*

an opponent may require the player to replay from within **(b)** **without penalty** but he must do so immediately – e.g. he cannot first go and see how the ball is lying (R11.4a);

– in *stroke play*

the original stroke is cancelled and he must replay from within the teeing ground plus **2 stroke penalty** and if he does not correct the error before playing from the next teeing ground – **disqualified** (R11.4b and D11.5/4)

2 if the ball is played but does not leave the teeing ground – it must be played it as it lies and may not re teed – if re teed **2 stroke penalty** (D11.3/2)

3 ball from tee hit out of bounds – a player may re tee anywhere in the teeing ground not necessarily as near as possible to where the previous stroke was played (D20.5/1)

4 if casual water covers the entire teeing ground part way through a competition the matter should be referred to the Committee who should relocate the teeing ground in match play. In stroke play they may first attempt to remove the water or suspend play until the teeing ground is playable (D25.1b/4) or relocate it if it can be done without undue advantage/disadvantage to other players

t5 TEMPORARY OBSTRUCTIONS

structures such as tents, grandstands etc. when declared in local rules to be moveable or immoveable obstructions by the Committee – see the local rules of the course and **Obstructions (o3)** for rules

t6 TESTING THE CONDITION

of the putting green – see **Putting green (p18)**
of a hazard – see **Bunker (b33)**, **Lateral water hazard (l1)** and **Water hazard (w2)**

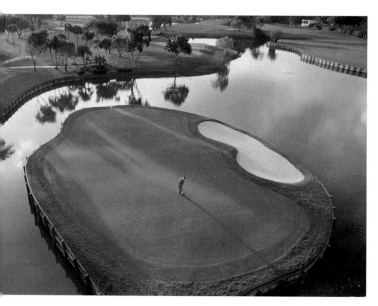

Turnberry Isle, Florida

t7 TEXAS SCRAMBLE

What is it?

a game for teams of 3 or 4. All players drive from the tee. They then select the best drive and all players play their second shot from that spot. This procedure continues until the hole is completed. Handicap allowances may be made in various ways e.g. the total handicap allowance for the team may apply or (more usually) a fraction of the total team handicap. It is applied by deducting it from the team score at the end of the round

Variations

1. **Ambrose Scramble** – the team must use at least 4 tee shots by each player

2. **Delaney Scramble** – the team may not choose more than 2 shots of any one player on each hole

3. **Drop Out Scramble** – the player whose ball is selected is not allowed to play the next shot

4. **Idaho Scramble** – the team must select the worst placed ball each time

What is it?

match play competition in which three play each other and each plays his own ball (DF) – see **Fourball (f9)** for general rules

Basic rules

the rules of golf apply but with the following variations because there are three separate matches being played:

1. if A's ball is touched by B, his caddie or equipment other than during a search for the ball – B incurs **1 stroke penalty** in his match against A **but not** in his match against C (R30.2a)

2. if a player's ball is deflected or stopped by an opponent, his caddie or equipment – **no penalty** and the player may either:
   (i) play it as it lies **or**
   (ii) cancel the stroke and play again from as near as possible to where cancelled stroke was played
   BUT in his match with the other opponent his ball must be played as it lies i.e. he can be playing two balls (R30.2b)

3. (i) if ABC play out of order in sequence BAC and A wants B to replay but C doesn't – B must play 2 balls for the hole – one from the original spot to satisfy A and the original ball from where it lies to satisfy C (D30.2/1)
   (ii) likewise if play is in order CAB and A and B disagree then C must play 2 balls
   (iii) if ABC play in order BAC and C wants B to replay but A doesn't, B continues with original ball because he has not played out of order vis-a vis C

TPC Scottsdale, Arizona

t9 THREESOME

What is it?

a game in which one plays against two and each side plays only one ball (DF)

Procedure

1 partners play strokes (a) alternately from the teeing ground and during the play of each hole (R29.1) – if an even number of strokes are played the same partner will putt into the hole and then play the next tee shot

2 playing in the wrong order (b) – **loss of hole/2 stroke penalty** (R29.2 and 3) plus in stroke play the error must be corrected before playing from the next teeing ground or if on the last hole before leaving the green – if not – **disqualified**

3 player accidentally moves his ball after address – **1 stroke penalty** but he must replay it, not his partner (D29.1/5)

> **(a) strokes**
> • penalty strokes are not deemed strokes for the purpose of the order of play
> • stroke played outside the teeing ground is not deemed a stroke for purposes of the order of play – the original player has to replay it, not his partner (D29.1/1)
> • if his partner does play it **penalty is 2 strokes** for playing outside the teeing ground **plus 2 strokes** for playing in the wrong order (D29.1/2)

4 composition of teams may not be changed after the first side has played from the tee (D29/1)

5 mixed team – man plays from the tee and goes out of bounds – the lady must play the next stroke from the men's tee (D29/2)

6 where Rules require a drop to be taken – the player to play the next stroke must drop the ball – even though the definition of player includes a partner in three/foursomes (D29.5)

7 either partner may sign the scorecard (D29/6)

8 a provisional ball must be played by the partner (D29.1/3)

b **wrong order**
• *partners drive in the wrong order for 3 holes in match play – error not noticed by opponents until the 3rd hole – opponents cannot claim first 2 holes because they should have realised the wrong order and time had passed to make a claim – they can claim the 3rd hole* (D29.2/2)

t10 THROUGH THE GREEN

the term used in the Rules to denote the whole area of the course except all hazards, the teeing ground and the putting green of the hole being played (DF)

t11 THROW OUT

a game in which in calculating the total score from their round the players can deduct the scores for their two worst holes

t12 THUNDER

see *Lightning* (l5)

t13 TIE

What is it?

the term when scores are equal at the end of the stipulated round

Basic rule

match play – the match should be continued hole by hole until won (app 1) (a)

stroke play – an 18 hole play off is recommended (app 1) but if not feasible a sudden death play off is recommended. If this is not feasible the result should be decided by a 'card' play off of the scores over the last 9 holes, or if still tied, the last 6 or then the the last 3. If the Committee does not prescribe a method then the players may agree one themselves (D33.6/4)

(a) **won**
• *a match believed to have been won is subsequently found to have been tied – the original result stands* (D2.3/1)

Basic rules

1 if a ball lies against a tree it must be played as it lies or declared unplayable – see **Ball unplayable (b23)** – and relief taken accordingly. For staked trees see **4**

2 there is no relief if a tree interferes with a players stance, line of play or area of intended swing unless provided by a local rule

3 tree wells tree stumps (D25/8) and fallen trees (D25/9) are part of the course and there is no relief if the ball lies in one (D33.2a/10.5) unless provided by a local rule

4 staked trees are often the subject of local rules permitting relief **without penalty** or may be marked as **Ground under repair** (see **(g9)**) check the local rules on the scorecard as these vary depending on whether trees are treated individually or as a group

5 a tree in a bunker is not part of the bunker (D13/2)

6 a tree in ground under repair is considered part of the ground under repair so a ball in the branches is within the gur even if it is in branches which hang outside the gur margin (D25/10) but not if it is in roots which extend outside the margin of the gur because the margin is deemed to extend downwards not upwards (D25.10/7)

7 if a tree falls into a fairway during a round the Committee may decide

(i) to do nothing and permit play to continue

(ii) to suspend play and have the tree removed

(iii) to declare the surrounding area ground under repair

(iv) to declare it a temporary obstruction and apply the appropriate local rule (D25.9/5)

Procedure

Procedure

1 ball in tree knocked out by outside agency – player unsure where the ball originally lay – replace it as near as possible if the ball can be played – if not declare the ball unplayable and proceed accordingly (D18.1/9) – see **Ball unplayable (b23)**

2 player climbs tree to play his ball and the ball is dislodged – **1 stroke penalty** (D18.2a/26)
BUT if the purpose of climbing the tree is merely to identify the ball with the intention of declaring it unplayable and the ball is dislodged – **no penalty** other than under the ball unplayable rule provided the intention to treat the ball as unplayable is announced (D18.2a/27)

3 if a tree is shaken by a player believing his ball is in it and the ball falls to the ground – **1 stroke penalty plus further 1 stroke penalty** if the ball is not replaced in the tree (D18.2a/28)
(if unable to replace the ball in the tree the player should declare the **Ball unplayable** (see **(b23)**) – **1 stroke penalty** – player may shake the tree to dislodge the ball **without penalty** if the purpose is to identify the ball in order to declare it unplayable (D18.2a/27))

Basic rules

t15 TROLLEY/GOLF CART

- part of a player's equipment when pulled/driven by a caddie
  – see *Caddie* (**c1**)
- when struck by a moving ball – see *Ball deflected – by player/opponent/fellow competitor* (**b8**)
- when as part of a player's equipment it strikes a ball – see *Ball moved – by player/opponent/fellow competitor* (**b18**)

Scottsdale, Arizona

UMBRELLA

- see *Assistance* (a13)

- when carried by a caddie – see *Caddie* (c1)

- when struck by a moving ball – see *Ball deflected – by player/opponent/fellow competitor* (b8)

- when as part of a player's equipment it strikes a ball – see *Ball moved – by player/opponent/fellow competitor* (b18)

- it may also be a *Moveable obstruction* (see (o3)) e.g. if it belongs to a spectator

 UNPLAYABLE LIE

see *Ball unplayable* (b23)

 UNDUE DELAY

see *Delay* (d3)

 USA

following revisions in the Appendices to the Rules as from 1st January 2000 there are no substantive differences between the application of the Rules in the USA and elsewhere in the world. A few minor decisions apply only in the USA and these are noted in the relevant sections of this book.

Left: TPC, Scottsdale, Arizona

W1 WATER

may be ***Casual water*** (see (**c4**)) or a
Lateral water hazard (see (**l1**)) or a
Water hazard (see (**w2**))

W2 WATER HAZARD

What is it?

any sea, lake, pond, river, ditch, surface drainage ditch or other open water course (whether or not containing water) or anything of a similar nature. The margin extends vertically upwards and downwards. Stakes and lines defining it are within it and should be yellow (a) (DF)

a defining
• stakes defining the boundary of a water hazard were wrongly placed and the water extended beyond the stakes – the boundary was deemed to be the natural extent of the water and not the stakes (D26/2)

Water hazard at San Lorenzo GC, Portugal

Basic rule ❶

if his ball lies in touches (b) or is lost (c) in a water hazard
a player is **under penalty** entitled to relief (R26.1)

(b) lies in a water hazard
• ball lands in a water hazard but is carried out of bounds by
the flow – it must be played under OB rules not water hazard rules
(D26.1/7)
• ball lands in out of bounds river but is carried in bounds by the flow –
as it comes to rest in bounds it must be played under the water
hazard rules and is deemed to have crossed the hazard at the
boundary of the course – even if it is in the middle of the river (D26.1/8)
• a ball is in the hazard if it breaks the vertical line upward from the
margin even though it may not be touching the ground e.g. if in a
tree overhanging the hazard (D26/1)
• if a ball last crosses the margin of a hazard where it is marked
as a water hazard but comes to rest in a part marked as a lateral
water hazard – relief must be taken as for a water hazard NOT as
for a lateral water hazard (D26.1/12)

(c) lost
• there must be reasonable evidence preponderantly in favour of
it being in the hazard that the ball is lost and not elsewhere –
otherwise lost ball rules under R27 apply (R26.1/D26.1/1) – see **Lost
ball (l10)**
• player searched for 1 minute and then considered his ball lost and
took relief under the water hazard rules – he then found his original
ball – if the evidence were deemed reasonable as to loss then he
must play his second ball in any event; if the search time was
considered too short and therefore the presumption of loss was not
reasonable the second ball was played from a **Wrong place** (see
(w9)) – loss of hole/2 stroke penalty plus 1 stroke penalty for
playing from a wrong place and the ball must then be played from
where the original ball was last played – if not, **disqualified** (D26.1/3)

Penalty

for breach of the rules –
loss of hole/2 strokes

Basic rules

Basic rule ❷

before making a stroke at a ball in or touching a water hazard a
player **must not** (R13.4):

    (i) test the condition of the hazard or any similar hazard

    (ii) touch the water with his club – even in the backswing

    (iii) touch the ground ⓐ in the hazard with a club or hand

    (iv) touch or move any loose impediment in or touching the
hazard

> ⓐ **ground**
> • *a bridge over a water hazard is an obstruction and
> the player may ground his club on it at address or in the
> backswing (D13.4/30) – an obstruction is not ground in a
> hazard but the ball is deemed in the hazard – (see **(03)**)*

Penalty

for breach of **basic rule ❷ loss of hole/2 strokes**

Water hazard, Mauni Lani GC, Hawaii

What is it?

Exceptions to Basic rule ❷

1. the player may touch the ground
   (i) as a result of or to prevent himself falling or to help him get into or out of the hazard (D13.4/3.5)
   (ii) in removing an obstruction
   (iii) in measuring
   (iv) in retrieving, lifting, placing or replacing a ball under the Rules

2. if the lie of a player's ball is affected by something after it came to rest (e.g. a divot from another player's stroke) the player may remove it **without penalty** as he is entitled to his original lie (D13.4/18)

3. the stakes defining a water hazard are obstructions – see **Obstructions (o3)** for relevant rules and procedures

4. rules permitting lifting, cleaning and identifying the ball do not apply in a water hazard (R12.2) **except** when searching for a ball in a hazard

Lost City GC, South Africa

Procedure

Procedure

the player may either:

1 play the ball as it lies **without penalty** (b)

or

2 take a **1 stroke penalty** and:

> **(i)** play as near as possible from the spot where the original ball was played (c)

or

> **(ii)** drop a ball any distance behind the hazard (d) on the extension of the line from the hole through the point where the ball last crossed (e) the margin of the hazard

(b) **as it lies**
• moving ball in a water hazard – **no penalty** if the player plays it (R14.5)

(c) **where original ball was played**
• player played over a water hazard into a greenside bunker – then hit against the side of the bunker and back into the water hazard – under **2** (i) he could drop in the bunker even though it was nearer the hole (D26.1/6)

(d) **behind the hazard**
• means on the opposite side of the hazard from the hole (D26.1/15)

What is it?

Basic rules

Exceptions

3 if the ball played from a water hazard comes out of the hazard but is unplayable, lost or goes out of bounds the player may take a **1 stroke penalty** and:

(i) drop as near as possible in the hazard to the spot from where the previous stroke was played **or** take a

further 1 stroke penalty and:

(ii) adopt Procedure **2** (ii)

or

(iii) play as near as possible from the spot where his last stroke outside the hazard **f** was played

e **last crossed**
• where it is not possible to determine where it last crossed the margin only option 2(i) is available (D28/4.5)

f **outside the hazard**
• means that the ball can in certain circumstances be dropped on the same side of the hazard as the hole (D26.1/15)

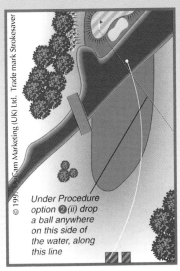

© 1997 DanCom Marketing (UK) Ltd. Trade mark Strokesaver

*Under Procedure option **2** (ii) drop a ball anywhere on this side of the water, along this line*

12th hole, Augusta, Georgia

under Procedure option **2** (i) the player may take the **1 stroke penalty** and play his third stroke from the teeing ground

or

under Procedure option **2** (ii) drop a ball anywhere behind the hazard along the extension of the line from the hole through the point where the ball last crossed the margin of the hazard

Procedure

371

Procedure

4 if a ball played from a water hazard remains in the hazard the player may adopt the Procedure **3** options

5 if pursuant to Procedure **3** or **4** the player opts to play from the spot in the hazard from where the previous stroke was played he may elect not to play his dropped ball and take a **further 1 stroke penalty** and adopt Procedure **3** (ii) or (iii)

6 where a ball is required to be dropped it may not be placed – e.g. if dropping would result in it rolling further into the hazard – relief should be taken under one of the other options (D26.1/10)

7 searching for a ball in a water hazard – a player may probe with a club or otherwise and there is **no penalty** if the ball is moved (**g**) but it must be replaced unless the player opts to take relief under **2** or **3** on page 370–371 (R12.1)

8 if a player in a water hazard takes inappropriate relief as if for a lateral water hazard he is penalised **loss of hole/2 strokes** for playing from the wrong place plus in stroke play **a further 1 stroke** for breach of the water hazard procedure (D26.1/11) – he must then adopt the correct procedure – if not – he is **disqualified**

What is it?

Basic rules

Procedure

g **moved**
• player who rotated a ball in a water hazard for the purpose of identifying it was **penalised 1 stroke** under R18.2a (see **Ball moved (b18)**) for touching it (D12.2/3)
• if he kicks it when searching this is not deemed pursuant to probing – **1 stroke penalty and replace it** (D12.1/5)

W3 WHITE

- **white posts/stakes** delineate areas which are *Out of bounds* (see **(o5)**)

- **white lines** may delineate areas which are *Ground under repair* (see **(g9)**) or *Out of bounds* (see **(o5)**)

- **white tee markers** indicate the mens medal tees

Lateral water hazards (see **(l1)**) should have red lines and/or stakes *Water hazards* (see **(w2)**) should have yellow lines/stakes

W4 WIND

is **not** an *Outside agency* (see **(o6)**)

Basic rule

if a ball is moved by the wind it must be played as it lies

Penalty

for picking up and replacing the ball in its original position – **1 stroke** and the ball should be replaced where the wind had blown it (R18.2) – see *Ball moved when stationary* (**b18**)

W5 WINTER RULES

an alternative name for the local rules which permit preferred lies – see *Preferred lie* (**p13**) for details

see *Loose impediments* (see **(l9)**)

W7 WRONG BALL

What is it?

any ball except the player's *Ball in play* (see **(b12)**), a *Provisional ball* (see **(p16)**) or in stroke play a *Second ball* (see **(s5)**) **a** (DF)

a **wrong ball**
  • *ball lifted on the putting green put to one side – the player then played it without having replaced it – as the ball was out of play it is a wrong ball (D15/4) a **loss of hole/2 stroke penalty** & in stoke play he must correct the error or **disqualified***
  • *player believed his original ball lost and played a provisional – he then played a wrong ball believing it to be the provisional but found the original and played it – **loss of hole/2 stroke penalty** (D15/7) **NB** penalties incurred with a provisional ball are usually cancelled if the original is found and played but the ball played in this instance was not the provisional – it was a wrong ball*
  • *ball changed during the play of a hole because it was identical to an opponent's ball – second ball is not a wrong ball but a wrongly substituted ball – (D15/6.5) **loss of hole/2 stroke penalty plus 1 stroke** for illegal lifting of the ball*

Basic rule

a player must hole out with the ball he played from the teeing ground **b** unless otherwise permitted by the Rules (R15.1)

b **ball played from the teeing ground**
  • *balls inadvertently exchanged by players between holes so they hit each other's from the next tee – **no penalty** because they are permitted to change balls between the play of holes*

Penalty

loss of hole/2 strokes if strokes are played (C) with the wrong
ball (d) (R15.1)

Exception

no penalty when a wrong ball is played in a *Bunker* (see (**b33**)),
Lateral water hazard (see (**l1**)) or *Water hazard* (see (**w2**)) (R15.2)

C played
• *player finds his ball and
declares it unplayable under Rule
28 – having dropped
it he then discovers it is not his –*
no penalty *as the act of dropping
is not deemed playing
a wrong ball (D15/13)*
• *if the stroke misses the wrong ball
– loss of hole/2 stroke penalty
(D15/1)*
• *even if wrong ball played is part of
a broken abandoned ball i.e. not a
whole ball –* **loss of hole/2 stroke
penalty** *(D15/3)*
• *even if the wrong ball is not in play
e.g. out of bounds –* **loss of
hole/2 stroke penalty** *plus if the
correct ball is OB additional* **1
stroke penalty** *to comply with OB
rules (D15/6)*

d application of penalty
• *two wrong balls played
in succession – player
plays correct ball third
time – only* **one 2
stroke penalty** *applied
(D15.3b/2)*

Procedure

Exceptions

Procedure

1 *match play* – if a player plays a wrong ball he loses the hole (e)

2 *stroke play* – the competitor must correct his mistake by playing the correct ball before playing a stroke from the next teeing ground (or before leaving the green if at the last hole) – if not – **disqualification** (R15.3)

3 strokes played with a wrong ball do not count in a player's score (R15.3) even in a hazard (R15.3) (f)

4 time spent in playing a wrong ball is not counted in the 5 minutes allowed under the Rules to search for a lost ball (DF)

(e) **match play procedure**
 • *if both players accidentally play each others ball then the first to have played with a wrong ball loses the hole. If this can't be determined – must play out the hole with wrong balls and the scores count (R15.2)*
 • *wrong ball played in error to green – opponent then concedes the hole – concession is not valid as the player lost the hole when the wrong ball was played (D2.4/9)*
 NB *concession stands if the wrong ball was played from a hazard (D2.4/9.5)*
 • *player wins hole but realises at the next hole that he is playing a wrong ball – opponent can claim the previous hole even though the player was not aware of the penalty (D9.2/8)*
 • *player A informs opponent B that B has played a wrong ball, B concedes the hole and loses the match. A subsequently establishes he had played the correct ball and B had given wrong information.*
 No penalty *and result stands as* **Wrong information** *(see* **(w8)***) refers to strokes taken (D9.2/11)*

What is it?

Basic rules

Penalty

Exceptions

1 when the player substitutes a ball in accordance with the Rules **(g)** it is not a wrong ball (R15.1)

2 when a player is playing a wrong ball and it is not known when the exchange took place – it is deemed to have taken place between holes unless there is evidence to the contrary – **no penalty** (D15.1/2)

3 when a wrong ball was played in error and the original ball was in the hole – **no penalty** (D1.1/4)

4 if the competitor has played a wrong ball because of the act of his fellow competitor – **no penalty** **(h)**

5 **no penalty** against a partner if a wrong ball is played in *Best ball/Fourball match play* (see **(f9)**)

f **in a hazard**
• *wrong ball played from bunker knocks fellow competitor's ball into the hole* – **no penalties** – *fellow competitor must replace and replay* (D18.5/1)

g **substitutes**
• *if a player substitutes another ball when not permitted it is not a wrong ball – it becomes the ball in play and if the error is not corrected under R20.6 – see **Substituting a ball (s31)** – loss of hole/2 stroke penalty*

h **act of fellow competitor**
• *player A marks B's ball and places it on the green, B unaware that it has been marked putts the ball as it lies – **no penalty**; if mistake realised the ball should be placed on the correct spot and played again; if not realised the score counts with the wrong ball* (D15.3b/3)

W8 WRONG INFORMATION

Basic rules

1 there is no specific rule prohibiting a player from deliberately giving wrong information but it is generally deemed to be contrary to the spirit of the game and the Committee would be justified in imposing the **disqualification penalty** (a) (R34.1)

2 in match play
(a) if wrong information is given as to the number of strokes taken there is **no penalty** provided the player corrects the mistake before his opponent plays his next stroke or if after completing the last hole, before leaving putting green (a). If not – provided the opponent makes a valid claim – **loss of hole penalty** (R9.2)
(b) failure to declare a penalty is deemed giving wrong information (R9.2) – **loss of hole penalty** provided the opponent makes a valid claim
(c) if a valid claim is not made the result of the match can only be adjusted subsequently if the offender knowingly gave wrong information (D2.5/9)

3 in *stroke play* there is **no penalty** for giving wrong information as to the number of strokes taken (b) (D9.3/1)

4 incorrect information regarding rules is not wrong information (D2.5/10)

5 wrong information given by a caddie or partner is deemed given by the player (D9.2/1)

a application of rule – match play

• *player A advises opponent B of the wrong score, B realises the error but does not correct A as it is to his advantage. B wins the match.* **No penalty** *under Rule 9.2 but the Committee could* **disqualify** *B under Rule 33.1 as behaving contrary to the spirit of the game* (D9.2/12)

• *player A declares 6 and B also scores 6. A realises his score was 5 and informs B before playing from the next tee – A wins the hole and* **no penalty** (D9.2/14)

• *wrong information was given which resulted in a player lifting his ball marker believing he had won the hole – the act of lifting was deemed to be the next stroke so his opponent could not then correct the mistake* (D9.2/5)

• *wrong information discovered several holes later –* **loss of hole penalty** *is applied and the match score adjusted accordingly* (D9.2/9)

b application of rule – stroke play

• *in stroke play sudden death play off, player A asks B his score and B wrongly claims 4. A has played 5 and picks up his ball –* **no penalty** *against B* (D9.3/1). *A has* **1 stroke penalty** *for lifting the ball without marking it and so loses the hole* (R20.1)

W9 WRONG PLACE

What is it?

the rules are restricted to dealing with situations after a ball has been dropped or placed (see Basic rule ❶) and when a ball is played from the wrong teeing ground (see Basic rule ❷ overleaf)

Basic rules

Procedure

Basic rule ❶

match play

> (i) when a ball is played from the wrong place after being
> dropped or placed – **loss of hole penalty** (R20.7a)

stroke play

> (i) when a ball is played from the wrong place after being
> dropped or placed or is not replaced having been moved –
> there is **no penalty** for playing from the wrong place – but
> there will almost certainly be a **2 stroke penalty** for not
> replacing the ball correctly or for some other offence under
> the rules relating to dropping, placing and replacing (a)
> (ii) there will be a **2 stroke penalty** if he breaches the
> procedural requirements on page 381 (R20.7b)

Basic rule ❷

when a ball is played from the **wrong teeing ground**
in **match play**

> an opponent may require the player to replay from within
> **without penalty** but he must do so immediately – e.g.
> he cannot first go and see how the ball is lying (R11.4a)

in **stroke play**

> the original stroke is cancelled and he must replay from
> within the correct teeing ground plus **2 stroke penalty** and
> if he does not correct the error before playing from the next
> teeing ground – **disqualified** (R11.4b and D11.5/4)

What is it?

Procedure

1 in *stroke play* if the player becomes aware of the error before playing from the next teeing ground **(b)** (or before leaving the green if at the last hole) and the breach is serious **(c)** e.g. he plays from a spot much nearer the hole, he should play a second ball from the correct place and then report the situation to the Committee who if the breach was considered serious will add a **2 stroke penalty** to the score with the second ball – but if the player fails to report to the Committee or adopts the wrong procedure – **disqualified**

2 if the breach is not serious then the score with the ball played from the wrong place counts plus the appropriate penalty (R20.7b)

a some other offence
• *player's ball hit maintenance vehicle and went out of bounds – player dropped his ball back in bounds by the vehicle – **2 stroke penalty** for breach of out of bounds rule plus a **further stroke and distance penalty** to comply with the **Out of bounds** (see **(o5)**) procedure (D20.7/1)*

b next teeing ground
• *the next one actually played not necessarily the next one in the correct sequence (D11.5/1)*

c serious
• *player loses sight of his shot and believes it to be in a bunker – he cannot find it and drops another ball in the bunker and plays it – the original ball is then found behind the green – he should have replayed from the spot of his original shot; dropping in the bunker was well in advance of the place of his previous shot – serious breach so **disqualified** (D20.7b/3) – provided he had not played from the next teeing ground he should have gone back to the original spot and replayed from there and added a **3 stroke penalty***
• *ball deflected out of bounds by maintenance vehicle – player simply dropped ball by vehicle and continued without penalty – he should have played from where the original ball was last played plus **3 stroke penalty** – but as the breach was serious – **disqualified** (D20.7/1)*

381

y1 YELLOW

- **yellow lines/stakes** delineate the boundaries of **Water hazards** (see **(w2)**)

- **yellow tee markers** define the mens forward medal tees/visitors tees

Above: after the round and when The Golf Rules Dictionary has been put away.....

Photo credits

The author gratefully acknowledges the invaluable assistance of Gary Braid of Angles for the specific rules photography, Longshot Golf Holidays for the numerous photos of the destinations featured in their holiday brochures, Michael Taylor of Portal Golf & Country Club for the use of the course for location shots and of the following for the use of their photography on the pages mentioned:

Emirates Hills GC Dubai 38, 39

Fairmont Canadian Pacific Hotels 54, 81, 116, 172, 262,358

Golf Links International 72, 104, 125, 149, 161, 188, 196, 206, 253, 345, 355, 363

Hyatt Hotels 11, 52, 112, 139, 163, 176, 181, 184, 204, 312, 352, 368

Longshot Golf Holidays 22, 26, 56, 87, 94, 105, 117, 137, 153, 167, 168, 197, 214, 232, 233, 239, 257, 259, 260, 278, 281, 289, 296, 302, 304, 308, 309, 348, 362, 364, 366, 382, 383

O'ahu Visitors Bureau 21

Scottsdale Visitors and Convention Bureau 361

Strokesaver/DuCann Marketing (UK) Ltd 102, 213, 247, 371

Sun International 59, 142, 194, 245, 305, 316, 369

The Palmilla Hotel 98, 250, 318

The Turnberry Hotel 51

Wyndham Hotel Rose Hall Jamaica 316, 317